THE TRIAL OF
J E S U S
OF NAZARETH

By MAX RADIN

PROFESSOR OF LAW IN THE
UNIVERSITY OF CALIFORNIA

THE LAWBOOK EXCHANGE, LTD.
Clark, New Jersey

ISBN 978-1-58477-662-8

Lawbook Exchange edition 2006, 2019

The quality of this reprint is equivalent to the quality of the original work.

THE LAWBOOK EXCHANGE, LTD.
33 Terminal Avenue
Clark, New Jersey 07066-1321

*Please see our website for a selection of our other publications
and fine facsimile reprints of classic works of legal history:*
www.lawbookexchange.com

Library of Congress Cataloging-in-Publication Data

Radin, Max, 1880-1950.
  The trial of Jesus of Nazareth / Max Radin.
    p. cm.
  Originally published: Chicago : University of Chicago Press,
    c1931.
  Includes index.
  ISBN 1-58477-662-5 (alk. paper)
  1. Jesus Christ--Trial. I. Title.

BT440.R3 2006
232.96'2--dc22   2005002840

Printed in the United States of America on acid-free paper

THE TRIAL OF
J E S U S
OF NAZARETH

By MAX RADIN

PROFESSOR OF LAW IN THE
UNIVERSITY OF CALIFORNIA

THE UNIVERSITY OF CHICAGO PRESS
CHICAGO · ILLINOIS

COMPOSED AND PRINTED BY THE UNIVERSITY OF CHICAGO PRESS
CHICAGO, ILLINOIS, U.S.A.

TO MY FRIEND
HENRY RAND HATFIELD

PREFACE

Whether this book has the substance of learning must be determined by those who read it. That it lacks the apparatus of learning may be noted with relief by laymen and with displeasure by scholars. I have none the less the temerity to submit it to the judgment of the latter group as well as of the former.

A huge volume would have barely sufficed if I had sought to digest the opinions proffered by scholars on the questions raised in the following pages. To examine these opinions critically and to estimate them would have expanded such a volume into a formidable treatise. If I have foregone this attempt, it is not because the judgments of scholars on this matter are valueless, but because in most cases their conclusions are the results of processes which the layman is not invited to estimate and in which the authority of an established scholarly tradition plays too great a part.

All the evidence we have of the events discussed is here presented. And it is presented completely, together with the discussion itself, so that no reference outside of the book is necessitated. When an assertion is made which contradicts current handbooks or even the consensus of opinion, I must beg my readers to believe it is made deliberately, and that, whether wrong or right, it is based upon an independent examination.

MAX RADIN

BERKELEY, CALIF.
April 2, 1931

TABLE OF CONTENTS

INTRODUCTION

Some forty years after Julius Caesar was murdered in the senate house at Rome a little boy was born in a tiny village near the southeastern corner of the shores of the Mediterranean. About this boy more stories have been told than of any other human being with the possible exception of the prince Siddhattha Gotama whom later ages were to call the Buddha, or perhaps Alexander, son of Philip, king of the Macedonians. One of these stories tells how he came to die, and it is with this story that we shall concern ourselves in the following pages.

How familiar the story is we need hardly say. It is likely that half the members of the human race, whether they are Christian or not, have heard of Jesus; and if they have heard of him at all, they have heard how he died on the cross by the judgment of a Jewish court or a Roman judge or both, nineteen hundred years ago. Not only have so many millions heard of this story, but literally thousands have examined it, discussed it, and written about it for many purposes and in many ways. Most of all, of course, Christian theologians have dealt with it—all sorts of theologians, orthodox and critical, for edification and for disputation.

But not only theologians have done so. It is a historical subject and in part at least it is a legal subject. Lay historians have therefore discussed it and not a few lawyers. But many others who were not theologians, preachers, historians, or lawyers have in latter days busied themselves with it. Obviously it is a story of absorbing interest and would be, for that reason alone, enormously important, if it had no religious implications whatever.

Its importance in Christian communities is natural. The death of Jesus is, in Christian contemplation, the supreme sacrifice whereby God redeemed man who but for this death would be eternally and irrevocably doomed. The trial of Jesus, ending in his condemnation and execution, was an essential step in the sacrifice, the Passion, to give it its theological name. To Christians who believed that this was so, every detail of this process was overwhelmingly important and there could be no such thing as an excessive interest or absorption in it. And those Christians who took the account as essentially true, but permitted themselves to question the truth or importance of particular details, were none the less concerned to know as much of these details as could be known. Finally, in the case of many who had ceased to be Christians, the traditions of Christian training or origin are extremely strong and the personality of Jesus retains a great deal of its sanctity.

If in spite of all this it is possible without impertinence or futility to examine this event again and again, it must be because there are elements in it which must be constantly revalued. And if a new attempt does no more than to place a new and different emphasis on certain points of the story, that may be a sufficient justification.

What took place at the trial of Jesus? How shall we go about finding out? Evidently there are two methods—the two methods which have in fact been employed in those many books and studies and accounts of which I have spoken. The choice of a method is intimately connected with our attitude to the documents which purport to describe the event from the testimony of eyewitnesses. The most important of these documents are what we

call the "four gospels," known by the traditional names of Matthew, Mark, Luke, and
John. Each one presents a fairly complete
narrative of the Passion. The gospels, however, also tell a great deal more. They describe persons and depict a society that in
part we know from other sources, some of
these sources being ancient books, some being
actual remains of the period—buildings, inscriptions, papyri, coins, and the like.

Now, we can deal with our sources after
the method which has most frequently been
adopted. We can start with the assured conviction that the gospel narratives are true, all
of them, not only in a spiritual sense but also
in a literal and concrete sense; that any person
who was present in Jerusalem on the days indicated would have seen precisely all the events
there described. So convinced, we have no
choice but to reconcile the apparent contradictions in the various narratives, if such are
brought to our attention. And if any fact
learned from sources outside the gospels seems
to contradict or qualify these, we must either
make a further reconciliation or reject this
outside material as false.

That is the method of faith and its result is

edification. But it is not the method of history.

That method requires us to treat the principal sources, the four gospel narratives, as though they were four newly discovered books dealing with persons and things wholly unrelated to us. We must pretend that we gained our first knowledge of the name of Jesus or of Christianity from reading these books. Evidently we cannot hope to be completely successful in this way of approaching the subject for the simple reason that the persons and things are not wholly unrelated to us, and we have not just learned of the name of Jesus by reading the gospels. Yet unless we make a brave and determined effort to do this thing, to treat the gospels as though they were Buddhist scriptures or documents of Chinese dynastic history, any historical inquiry is vitiated at the outset. We must look at the evidence as it appears to us. If there seem to be contradictions, we must make up our minds whether we shall choose between them or attempt a reconciliation. And if we choose between contradictory statements, we must do so on the basis of the greater probability of one of them. For our purposes, the gospels are statements in a printed book of which we can trace the history up to a certain date and conjecture it beyond that.

This method is as different as it can be from the method of faith, and it must be clearly borne in mind that we cannot fuse the two. They exclude each other. It is important to say this because investigators of this or any other question must be warned that they cannot have it both ways. They cannot know in advance what is true and at the same time profess to be searching for it. It may well be that their advance knowledge is better than the knowledge their search would reveal. It is quite possible that their inherited faith is a better source of truth than historical inquiry. But it is a different source, and it is not altogether honest to go through the motions of groping for something we already have in our hands.

Therefore, in the following pages, we shall have to content ourselves with such an approximation to historical indifference as we can achieve. And our first attention must be directed to the fact that with the best will in the world we could not be completely successful in finding out what really happened at the trial of Jesus. Our evidence is fragmentary. Each of the gospels professes to give a complete account of the Passion, but it is complete only in outline, not in details. Our other sources, too, both in books and in archaeological data, give us only a few of the many facts we should like to have, if we wished to know ancient society as well as we know contemporary society. In other words, our evidence at its best is incomplete, and it would be so though we assumed that every statement in the gospels is an accurate and precise description of a historical fact, and though we made the same assumption about the statements in other books written at or near the time of Jesus.

Still if these assumptions might safely be made we should be fairly on in our task of reconstructing the event we have in mind. The difficulty is that we have undertaken to proceed without assumptions and we must take our pieces of evidence as they come to us.

Now, this attempt is in no sense new. Within the last two centuries a great many per- have tried to examine the evidence we are about to consider, and have tried to do so without making any assumptions. Curiously enough, they were for the most part devout

Christians who were brought up in childhood
to believe that the gospel narratives were true
before in their maturity they set themselves to
find out whether they were. We speak of them
as "Higher Critics," in which the words are
capitalized because they are almost technical
terms and denote men engaged in the precise
undertaking just referred to, the examination
of the gospels with a view to testing their
source, origin, and authenticity.

The results of their investigations are fairly
well known to cultivated modern men of the
Western world. On many matters they do not
agree at all, but on a number of them most of
them do agree. There is consequently a great
temptation to begin with their consensus and
take as established historical fact what New
Testament criticism declares to be so.

However, that will scarcely do. Doubtless,
critical theologians and those who adopt their
conclusions are free from the sort of bias which
the older-fashioned theologians not merely
have but boast of. Their conclusions have not
been presented in advance by religious dogma
or religious discipline. They know not merely
the gospels, but they know history, and they
are earnest men, most eager to arrive at the

truth, neither scoffers nor militant atheists.
Still it cannot be denied that there are other
disciplines besides those of religion. The methods of the critical school and the conclusions to
which they are declared to lead have themselves a history of several generations of university teaching. They are established, it almost seems, in a fashion very like the dogmas
of an organized church. Certainly a certain
measure of intolerance toward those who question them too closely is not altogether absent.
At any rate, their established position, the
tradition concerning them, the association of
the movement with efforts toward social and
political freedom, the reverence felt toward
the great personalities who pronounced them—
all these things may vitiate a historical investigation as much as dogma, and it is open to us
to wonder whether some of the historical statements made by this group of critics have not
in fact been so vitiated.

Consequently, we are not required to accept
even the unanimous agreement of scholars
without question, and if we feel ourselves com-
petent to judge their materials, we may insist
on knowing how such scholars arrived at the
conclusions they set forth.

We meet first of all the astounding fact that the reality of the event itself has been questioned. This was by no means first done when Professor Arthur Drews of Karlsruhe wrote his *Christ-Myth* in 1909, a book translated into English in 1911. Indeed, an American, Professor William Benjamin Smith of Tulane University, both before and after Drews's work, had quite independently reached conclusions which involved the denial of Jesus' historical existence and consequently of his trial and death. Smith's books and those of Drews are available and their arguments can be examined and valued. The most important of these arguments are that certain ancient writers who might normally be supposed to mention Jesus do not do so, and that parallels for the incidents recorded of Jesus can be found in stories about other personages at different times and places—stories which are almost certainly myths.

Without attempting to take up every part of the argument, we may reasonably reach the conclusion that it is far more probable that Jesus actually lived as a historical personage than that he did not. For one thing two Roman writers writing about A.D. 100 speak of the Christians as an organized group in Rome about A.D. 60. It is almost inconceivable that they invented the story and extremely unlikely that they were mistaken about the fact. We should therefore have to believe that thirty years after the supposed death of a man who never had lived, hundreds, perhaps thousands, of people not only believed firmly that he had lived, but at great danger to themselves believed him to have been divinely commissioned to establish a universal kingdom. This fundamental improbability certainly seems of greater weight than the silence of one or two writers who wrote a few years after Jesus. We must accordingly discard this extreme form of skepticism, and approach our problem with a certain confidence that the event we are trying to reconstruct in our imaginations really occurred.

Outside of the gospels we have one definite statement which it seems almost absurd to question. It is in the *Roman History* or *Annals* of Tacitus, written about A.D. 100. He states (xv. 44): "Christus, the originator of the sect called Christians, suffered capital punishment by command of the procurator, Pontius Pilatus, during the reign of Tiberius." This

must therefore have happened some time before March 16, A.D. 37, the day of Tiberius'
death, and, it seems to me, it places beyond
reasonable question the existence of Jesus, the
approximate date of his death, the fact of his
execution on a capital sentence, and the name
and office of his judge. Pilatus (Pilate) is never
elsewhere mentioned by any Roman writer,
but he is frequently mentioned in the Greek
works of two Jewish writers—Philo of Alexandria who was a younger contemporary of
Jesus and Josephus who wrote between the
years A.D. 70 and 90. Pilate was recalled to
Rome under charges just before the death of
Tiberius although we are not altogether sure
what the charges were. The several independent statements of Philo, of Josephus, and of
Tacitus fix the date of Pilate's governorship
and still further narrow the date of the death
of Jesus to the space between A.D. 26 and 36
since Pilate's administration lasted so long.

This fact, then, that between the years A.D.
26 and 36 the Roman governor of Judea, Pontius Pilate, ordered the execution of a provincial known to the Romans as "Christus" is the
only fact of the trial of Jesus which is practically unassailable, if we reject the *Myth*

hypothesis, as I think we must. We can add to that our knowledge, also derived from non-Christian sources, that "Christus" is a Greek word and that it is the translation of the Hebrew word *Mašiah*—which we know in the form of "Messiah" although this word happens to be derived from the Aramaic *Mešiha* rather than from the Hebrew. Now "Messiah" means "Annointed," and, again without going to Christian sources, we can be fairly sure that "Annointed" in this case was the particular "Annointed One" who was eagerly awaited by both Jews and non-Jews in this region and who it was hoped would by divine command establish some form of permanent theocracy over the whole world.

This much we can gather from the sentence in Tacitus and the passages alluded to in the other writers—mostly Jewish—of about that time. It is not a great deal but it is something to begin with.

All other information that we have comes from Christian sources and therefore to that extent must be examined critically. This does not in the least mean that the sources are suspect. It merely means that those who prepared these documents did not receive the statements in them critically but accepted with enthusiastic faith anything in them which would glorify the person of Jesus, and would lower the persons and character of his opponents, especially those who were instrumental in causing his death. Further, most of the documents may have had a controversial purpose within the Christian church itself and the details contained may have have been selected with a view to disproving or proving some particular theologic dogma.

That some of these documents were deliberately invented for one or the other of these reasons by the people who wrote them is extremely likely. About a great many of them this was the belief among Christians themselves even in ancient times. Documents of this character must accordingly be rejected out of hand as historical sources unless there is some reason to believe that the writers had access to documents and traditions now lost to us. We have no reason to believe it, however, for a certain number of books which we generally list as the "New Testament Apocrypha." The most striking example of these is the book called the Acts of Pilate, a late and clumsy forgery, devoid of merit even as a work of the imagination, although Mr. Papini has absurdly based a great deal of his *Life of Christ* on it. There are a great many others which we possess in more or less complete form, and some of them seem to be as old as the second, third, or fourth centuries A.D. However, we cannot use them whether they confirm or supplement what the gospels state.

If there were statements in them contradictory to the gospels, we should have to make up our minds whether the contradictions were really derived from lost sources or were hostile perversions of what we now have. For example, this latter explanation is almost certainly true for the few Jewish legends about the death of Jesus which we find in the Babylonian Talmud, a book which reached its present form outside the Roman Empire somewhere between A.D. 300 and 500. These statements have no historical value whatever and merely voice the bitter hostility existing between Jews and Christians at that time and place—a hostility which could not have been publicly expressed except in the non-Christian Persian Empire to which Babylon belonged.

But naturally such hostile perversions of the gospel accounts are not likely to be met with in Christian documents, even though some of these documents were written to maintain doctrines which the later church denounced as heretical. Or, at any rate, the contradictions, if they exist, are rather in tone and spirit than in concrete details.

We must then rely entirely on the gospel narratives. They form part of the New Testament—much the larger and more important part; they are, of course, easily available, and there is no single word in them that has not been examined and carefully studied many times. For many centuries they have been considered—as they are still considered by millions—the word of God which it was a dangerous offense to question or to misunderstand. It is necessary once more to remind ourselves that for our purposes we must make the difficult effort of forgetting the sanctity with which they have for so long been invested and must separate them, as much as we can, from the associations of holiness and awe in which most of us have first met them.

What are the gospels if we treat them as evidence? They are statements in a printed book which has passed through hundreds of editions since it was first published in the year

1611. In those editions the spelling has been gradually modernized, but no other change has taken place, and when we read what we call the Authorized or King James Version of the Bible we read it to all intents and purposes as the committee of divines and scholars of King James's time published it. And, as we all know, this book published—now more than three hundred years ago—professed to be a translation; in the part which concerns us, a translation from the Greek. It is true that the commission was in part guided by previous translations, one made in 1535 by Bishop Coverdale, and others made before and after 1535; but in the main they claim to have translated it directly and independently from a Greek book—a Greek printed book which we still have and can examine. This, too, had gone through a great many editions since its first publication in 1516 by the great Erasmus at Basel; but in this case the editions were not quite the same, and showed several discrepancies. We should not call them serious discrepancies, because they are generally about words and not about the general sense or the sequence of events, but in theological matters words are important and a great many violent disputes have been engaged in about whether this or that edition of the Greek New Testament is the better.

At any rate, when the commission translated the Bible in 1611, there were several texts in use, varying in details, and the text they selected was the result of a somewhat arbitrary judgment.

Where did the scholars who published the various Greek Testaments between 1516 and 1611 get their Greek text? This again we can answer with some certainty. There are a great many manuscripts in existence of the New Testament which run from the fourth to the fifteenth centuries. Some of them have been found recently, but most were known in the sixteenth century, and many of these could have been consulted by the editors of the Greek Bible. How many of these manuscripts actually were consulted by Erasmus and by Theodore Beza—who both made important editions—we cannot be sure, but we are pretty certain that they did not have access to a single manuscript which we do not now possess.

In fact, we can be fairly sure from documents of the time, that they really used only a small fraction of the hundreds of manuscripts which they might have used and which have been used by later editors. There are a great number of discrepancies between any or all of the sixteenth-century Greek Testaments and the Greek text which modern scholars have accepted after a careful and exhaustive study of several hundred manuscripts and a minute comparison of all of them.

We must remember that the famous Greek scholars of the sixteenth century, men like Erasmus and Beza, were in a sense pioneers in such matters as the study of manuscripts and of ancient life, although in genius and sheer learning they were probably greater than most of their successors. It has therefore been felt by Christian scholars that the English Bible ought to be made to conform to what we have every reason to believe is a closer approximation to the correct text of the gospels. There have accordingly been two revisions of the Authorized (King James) Version, one in England in 1881 and a later one in America in 1901. A great many English Bibles give one or the other of these versions, but there is no general agreement about this practice, and it may correctly be stated that the larger number of English Testaments to be found in homes and libraries are in the Authorized Version, with the Revised Version (R.V.) or the American Revised Version (A.R.V.) in the margins.

It may be said, however, that in the matters which concern us, the trial and execution of Jesus, there is not much difference between the Authorized and the later versions, so that the discrepancies between the various manuscripts, while serious and numerous enough for theological and doctrinal controversies, are of no great moment from the historical standpoint.

Now, as to the manuscripts themselves. The oldest manuscripts are two of the fourth century and three of the fifth century. That is to say, we could, at a pinch, get about the same story, even in detail, as the one in our current English Bible, if we used a parchment book which was written in Greek about the year A.D. 375, let us say. That is, of course, taking our testimony about what happened far back indeed, fifteen centuries and a half back of our own time and that much nearer to the time which the gospels purport to describe.

But even in A.D. 375 we are a considerable distance from the time of Jesus. Further, Christianity had already been the dominant religion for several generations. The emperors were Christian, and it was becoming a criminal offense to be unorthodox, although there was no universal agreement as to what was orthodox. If these old manuscripts had been originally composed then, they might represent a real tradition orally transmitted among Christians, but they might also have been pious inventions. There are other books written about that time which certainly are pious inventions and which no Christians at the present time regard as having the least historical value.

But our oldest manuscripts were certainly not composed in the fourth century when they were written. They are copies of older manuscripts. For one thing the five oldest do not agree exactly and no one of them seems to have been copied from any one of the others. They must all have been copied from older books. How faithfully they were copied we cannot know. We know the habits of manuscript-makers in those days, and we know that they took greater liberties than we like to take when we profess to be copying other books. But at all events we can only conjecture the exact text of the manuscripts from which our oldest existing manuscripts were copied, and it is from these, after a great deal of discussion and comparison and with some uncertainties and doubts about words, that, in the last analysis, our gospel evidence about the trial of Jesus comes to us.

How far can reasonable conjecture take us before A.D. 375? Surely a century, perhaps even two. At any rate, most men who have given their lives to the study of these matters agree that the four gospels Matthew, Mark, Luke, and John were in written form, nearly as we have them now, before the year A.D. 200. Their agreement does not preclude independent examination, and is certainly not a final determination. It is in any case based on a balance of probability and implies the exercise of a trained judgment.

Between this date, A.D. 200 and 33, the traditional date of the Crucifixion, the gospels took their present form. Each of the gospels has a history of its own. There is no good evidence that within that period they were ever published together in one book, and there is some evidence that Christians could write about A.D. 150 who had never heard of them. And there is a great deal of evidence that in the second and third centuries A.D. many other accounts, widely different from our own, were known and used. Not all Christians regarded our gospels in their present or their original form as more entitled to credit than other books, some of which we have in full and some of which we know by quotations in existing writings, and most of which have long ago been rejected as without historical value.

We must take our evidence, then, as we find it, as statements in Greek manuscript books of which the oldest are nearly three and a half centuries after the death of Jesus, and seem to be copies of books which cannot be traced back with any probability further than one century and a half after his death.

Who the authors of our gospels are we shall try to determine when we deal with them, or, better, we shall try to find out whether it can be determined. But as the opinion of scholars is widely divergent on these matters, and as it is necessary to refer to the gospels constantly by their familiar names, we must find some way of indicating that we are not prejudging the question. Matthew, Mark, Luke, and John were probably historical personages having the relation to Jesus which tradition gives them. That is, Matthew and John were contemporaries and disciples of Jesus, and Mark and Luke were younger men, not themselves disciples, but disciples of his disciples. To indicate the gospels it may be well to use these names with quotation marks; e.g. "Matthew," etc., whether or not we come to the conclusion that any one of the gospels is really the work of the man whose name we have been taught to attach to it.

There is one final preliminary consideration which is constantly neglected. It is the common practice to treat the details of the trial by fusing the accounts of the four gospels and citing now one and now another as authority. That is done even by critical investigators who do not treat the gospel narratives as inspired truth. It is unfortunate for our purposes, since it produces the impression that there is somewhere such a fused version extant and it seems to create a necessity of finding a place in this common version for the details mentioned in any one of them.

This, I think, is a capital error, and its abandonment seems to me in itself a justification for re-examining the evidence, if such justification is needed. These narratives are, as we find them, independent. No one refers to any other, and certainly no one expressly undertakes to supplement the other. Taken at their face value, they all undertake to tell us fully what took place, and no one is consciously omitting details of importance. It will be well to treat each story independently and to judge them independently, and one story cannot gain or lose in plausibility from conclusions we may come to about another.

We shall begin with "Mark" and not with "Matthew." There is a general agreement among critical scholars that "Mark" is the oldest of the gospels. It has undoubtedly several of the marks of age. It is the shortest, simplest, most direct—one might almost say, most naïve in its presentation. We shall first look at the gospel narrative as it is given in the Authorized Version and then see what we can learn from it.

CHAPTER I

MARK

14: 1. After two days was the feast of the passover, and of unleavened bread; and the chief priests, and the scribes, sought how they might take him by craft, and put him to death.

2. But they said, Not on the feast-day, lest there be an uproar of the people.

[Then follows the narrative of the preparation for the Passover supper with the disciples.]

10. And Judas Iscariot, one of the twelve, went unto the chief priests, to betray him unto them.

11. And when they heard it, they were glad, and promised to give him money. And he sought how he might conveniently betray him.

[The narrative of the supper follows.]

43. And immediately while he yet spake, cometh Judas, one of the twelve, and with him a great multitude with swords and staves, from the chief priests, and the scribes and the elders.

44. And he that betrayed him, had given them a token, saying, Whomsoever I shall kiss, that same is he; take him, and lead him away safely.

45. And as soon as he was come, he goeth straightway to him, and saith, Master, Master; and kissed him.

46. And they laid their hands on him, and took him.

47. And one of them that stood by, drew a sword, and smote a servant of the high priest, and cut off his ear.

48. And Jesus answered and said unto them, Are ye come out as against a thief, with swords and with staves to take me?

49. I was daily with you in the temple, teaching, and ye took me not; but the scriptures must be fulfilled.

50. And they all forsook him and fled.

51. And there followed him a certain young man, having a linen cloth cast about his naked body: and the young men laid hold on him.

52. And he left the linen cloth, and fled from them naked.

53. And they led Jesus away to the high priest: and with him were assembled all the chief priests, and the elders and the scribes.

54. And Peter followed him afar off, even into the palace of the high priest: and he sat with the servants, and warmed himself at the fire.

55. And the chief priests, and all the council, sought for witness against Jesus to put him to death; and found none.

56. For many bare false witness against him, but their witness agreed not together.

57. And there arose certain, and bare false witness against him saying,

58. We heard him say, I will destroy this temple that is made with hands, and within three days I will build another made without hands.

59. But neither so did their witness agree together.

60. And the high priest stood up in the midst, and asked Jesus, saying, Answerest thou nothing? what is it which these witness against thee?

61. But he held his peace, and answered nothing. Again the high priest asked him, and said unto him, Art thou the Christ, the Son of the Blessed?

62. And Jesus said, I am: and ye shall see the Son of man sitting on the right hand of power, and coming in the clouds of heaven.

63. Then the high priest rent his clothes, and saith, What need we any further witnesses?

64. Ye have heard the blasphemy: what think ye? And they all condemned him to be guilty of death.

65. And some began to spit on him, and to cover his face, and to buffet him, and to say unto him, Prophesy: and the servants did strike him with the palms of their hands.

15: 1. And straightway in the morning the chief priests held a consultation with the elders and scribes, and the whole council, and bound Jesus, and carried him away, and delivered him to Pilate.

2. And Pilate asked him, Art thou the King of the Jews? And he answering, said unto him, Thou sayest it.

3. And the chief priests accused him of many things: but he answered nothing.

4. And Pilate asked him again, saying, Answerest thou nothing? behold how many things they witness against thee.

5. But Jesus yet answered nothing; so that Pilate marvelled.

6. Now at that feast he released unto them one prisoner, whomsoever they desired.

7. And there was one named Barabbas, which lay bound with them that had made insurrection with him, who had committed murder in the insurrection.

8. And the multitude crying aloud, began to desire him to do as he had ever done unto them.

9. But Pilate answered them, saying, Will ye that I release unto you the King of the Jews?

10. (For he knew that the chief priests had delivered him for envy.)

11. But the chief priests moved the people that he should rather release Barabbas unto them.

12. And Pilate answered, and said again unto them, What will ye then that I shall do unto him whom ye call the King of the Jews?

13. And they cried out again, Crucify him.

14. Then Pilate said unto them, Why, what evil hath he done? And they cried out the more exceedingly, Crucify him.

15. And so Pilate, willing to content the people, released Barabbas unto them, and delivered Jesus, when he had scourged him, to be crucified.

16. And the soldiers led him away into the hall, called Pretorium; and they called together the whole band;

17. And they clothed him with purple, and platted a crown of thorns, and put it about his head.

18. And began to salute him, Hail, King of the Jews!

19. And they smote him on the head with a reed, and did spit upon him, and bowing their knees, worshipped him.

20. And when they mocked him, they took off the purple from him, and put his own clothes on him, and led him out to crucify him.

21. And they compel one Simon a Cyrenian, who passed by, coming out of the country, the father of Alexander and Rufus, to bear his cross.

22. And they bring him unto the place Golgotha, which is, being interpreted, The place of a skull.

23. And they gave him to drink, wine mingled with myrrh: but he received it not.

24. And when they had crucified him, they parted his garments, casting lots upon them, what every man should take.

25. And it was the third hour, and they crucified him.

26. And the superscription of his accusation was written over, THE KING OF THE JEWS.

27. And with him they crucify two thieves, the one on his right hand, and the other on his left.

28. And the scripture was fulfilled, which saith, And he was numbered with the transgressors.

29. And they that passed by, railed on him, wagging their heads, and saying, Ah, thou that destroyest the temple, and buildest it in three days.

30. Save thyself, and come down from the cross.

31. Likewise also the chief priests mocking, said

among themselves with the scribes, He saved others; himself he cannot save.

32. Let Christ the King of Israel descend now from the cross, that we may see and believe. And they that were crucified with him, reviled him.

33. And when the sixth hour was come, there was darkness over the whole land, until the ninth hour.

What inference may be drawn from this account by anyone who seriously tries to empty his mind of prepossessions?

Let us restate "Mark's" account in narrative form.

The ecclesiastical authorities of the Jews deliberately determine to commit a judicial murder in the case of Jesus. Before they had perfected their plan, Judas, one of the disciples, of his own accord proposed to the authorities to betray Jesus for money. The latter was thereupon arrested when he left his supper table on the night of the first day of the Passover. That same night he was brought to the house of the high priest who heard him with his Council. A number of perjured witnesses appeared against Jesus but these contradicted one another. One specific charge—the only one mentioned—was to the effect that he had boasted that he could tear down the Temple and re-erect it within three days. To this charge Jesus refused to plead. He was then asked whether he claimed to be the Messiah and the son of God. This he not only admitted but reasserted forcibly and announced a divine manifestation of the fact.

The high priest treated this as the confession of guilt on a capital charge and the Council unanimously voted to condemn him.

The following morning, after a consultation with his Council and other advisers, the high priest had Jesus taken to the Roman procurator, Pilate. Pilate's first question of Jesus was whether he claimed to be King of the Jews. This question Jesus did not specifically answer. The chief priests made many accusations and brought forward many witnesses. Pilate directed Jesus to answer the charges, but he did not do so.

The crowd about the tribunal clamored for the established privilege of having some condemned criminal released. Pilate offered to release Jesus whom he called "King of the Jews." The crowd rejected him, being urged thereto by the priests, assented to his execution and demanded Bar-Abbas, the condemned leader of a recently suppressed insurrection. Pilate resisted at first and finally yielded, giving orders that Jesus be first scourged and then crucified.

The Roman soldiers taunted him with the title "King of the Jews," which was later written over the cross. Passers-by, however, priests and populace, taunted him not with this title but with the alleged boast of being able to destroy and rebuild the Temple.

The foregoing is, I think, an accurate statement of what is contained in "Mark's" account, a statement given quite baldly, to which no comment has been added, except those made by "Mark" himself.

One point stands out. In the opinion of the writer, Jesus was illegally condemned. Not only were the witnesses perjured, but the charge, even if true, would not have justified condemnation. The high priest and his chief associates, who constituted part of the court which condemned Jesus, had themselves, in "Mark's" opinion, suborned the witnesses and trumped up the charges. Pilate would have been glad to pardon him, but the crowd, whose acclamation was needed, preferred a popular insurgent chief, one Bar-Abbas. Jesus is therefore represented as the innocent victim of a conspiracy on the part of the ecclesiastical authorities, a victim who lost his only chance of safety through the preference of a ruffianly mob for a man who appealed more to their sympathies.

The other point which is apparent is that Pilate, the Roman procurator, who gave the order for Jesus' execution, is really cleared of any direct responsibility for his death. The weight of the blame is placed quite clearly on the shoulders of the priests, the Council, and the mob, and not on those of the Roman officials. The soldiers, to be sure, are charged with extreme brutality, but "Mark" may have expected his readers to know, as was the fact, that Roman soldiers were likely to be recruited anywhere and not to be properly Romans. It is true that Pilate attempted to elicit from Jesus the admission that he had assumed the royal title, and it is also true that he asks Jesus rather sharply why he does not reply to the accusations against him. Still, while there is no statement that Pilate had any good will toward his prisoner, there is a plain assumption that he had no ill will. He twice makes a distinct effort to save him.

Now, "Mark" does not claim to be an eye-

witness, but he speaks as though his information may have come from eyewitnesses. Can
we distinguish between what is their evidence
and what is their opinion as transmitted to us
by the writer?

How did anyone come to know that there
had been a corrupt bargain between Judas and
the priests? The loyalty of Judas may have
been suspected and the fact of his treason may
have been apparent, although to an outside
observer of the events which "Mark" relates
even the betrayal would be an inference. But
who made public the actual offer and acceptance between Judas and his employers? It is
not the sort of thing that the parties themselves do, even if they think of it as a regretta-
ble means to a desirable end. It is conceivable
that they avowed their conduct with cynical
effrontery. But there is no word said to help
us to suppose so, and we have also to consider
as a possible explanation that the story of the
bargain is an inference with which "Mark's"
informant pieced together the certain facts:
the fact that Jesus was arrested immediately
after Judas had greeted him with a kiss. In
the story of the Supper as "Mark" gives it
Jesus does not unmistakably denounce Judas

as his betrayer, but uses veiled and general
language, so that, if "Mark's" informant was
a disciple, he might not have known with certainty whom Jesus had had in mind until the
moment of the arrest.

Then, there is the other conspiracy, that
among the priests themselves to arrest and
condemn Jesus on the Passover. Must we suppose that some one of the conspirators later
repented and told of it or that someone boasted
of it? We shall have to make a large use of this
particular hypothesis to sustain the eyewitness
character of "Mark's" informant. Or, again,
shall we take it to be an inference which was
drawn from the assurance of Jesus' innocence
together with what seemed to "Mark's" informant an arbitrary judgment coupled with
flagrant and obvious perjury?

A third point is the statement that Pilate
was convinced of Jesus' innocence. Pilate does
not say this in so many words at the time.
There is no suggestion that Pilate later announced his belief as he is made to do in later
legends. We may again consider it an inference. To be sure, it would seem a highly probable inference to an observer who noted two
successive attempts of the Roman governor to

spare his life, but it is not, after all, the only possible inference.

If these inferences are temporarily disregarded, is it possible to consider others? The account in "Mark" is that of an indignant follower who sees his beloved master wrongfully killed. What is the best case one could make out for the high priest on the same facts as those which "Mark" reports as facts? Is the following version of the events inconsistent with them?

The high priest heard that Jesus was present in Jerusalem. Accusations were brought to him that this man had made statements or done acts which under existing Jewish law constituted a capital offense. He thereupon ordered his arrest, which was achieved by inducing one of Jesus' followers to betray him.

The high priest, thinking the matter urgent, had Jesus arraigned at once at a night meeting of his Council which was also a court. A very large number of witnesses appeared. The high priest found only two charges sufficiently important to be dwelt on. One was the charge that Jesus had boasted of his power to destroy the Temple and rebuild it miraculously. That might be a charge of magic or of religious imposture. Either was capital. Jesus, however, did not admit the truth of it and the testimony was not completely satisfactory.

The second charge was that Jesus had claimed to be the Messiah. That was, in the high priest's eye, both religious imposture and treason. This claim Jesus reiterated in open court. He was accordingly formally condemned and brought the next morning to the Roman governor to have the capital sentence confirmed and executed.

Is there anything in the narrative of "Mark" outside of what must be, or are likely to be, the inferences of "Mark's" informant, which is inconsistent with this view of the high priest? I think it must be admitted that there is not. That is to say, the high priest may not have been at all a corrupt, crafty, and tyrannical man, but a conscientious official enforcing existing law against a man he honestly deemed to be a dangerous criminal, convicted of crime on his own confession.

Let us take care, however, not to suppose that this inference concerning the high priest's attitude and character is in any sense better supported than the opinion and inference which "Mark" presents. Even if we assume that the tradition which "Mark" gives was at two or three removes from eyewitnesses, it was at least, to that extent, much nearer than any of our guesses can possibly be. There is accordingly somewhat more evidence for "Mark's" inference than for this one, since even at third hand "Mark's" Gospel claims to be a record of how the physical appearance and acts of the high priest impressed those who saw him, and about these things we cannot even hazard a guess. At the same time it was an impression produced on highly and passionately excited persons incapable of believing ill of their leader or good of those who harmed him. We may have occasion later to confirm or reject either "Mark's" inferences or any other proposed in whole or in part.

Now as to Pilate. Suppose we assume the following:

Pilate received the Jewish ecclesiastical authorities in his residence, that is, seated on his chair of office. Jesus was then arraigned before him. Before any accusation was presented Pilate asked Jesus at once whether he had assumed the title of "King of the Jews." Such an assumption was necessarily a denial of Roman sovereignty. The title of "king"—even

the minor royalties such as tetrarch or eth-
narch—negatived direct government by a
Roman official. No kingdom could lie within
the *provincia*, the range of activities of a
Roman procurator or even a pro-consul. There
could be kings who were allies and vassals of
the Roman state, but their titles depended
upon recognition by the Senate or by the imperator. If Jesus had admitted the assumption
of a royal title, Pilate would have had before
him a confessed rebel.

But Jesus evaded the question, and neither
admitted nor denied it. Pilate thereupon heard
the charges brought by the priests. These
were many and were supported by many witnesses. The fact that there were witnesses
seems to indicate that Pilate had not dropped
the charge that the royal title had been assumed, and it may be that these witnesses asserted that such assumption had been made.
Whatever it was that they testified to, Jesus
refused to reply although particulary called
upon to do so.

Nothing is said of the fact that the high
priest and Council had already condemned
him on a capital charge. Pilate apparently
had the legal power to enforce that condemna-

tion by the death penalty. Let us assume that
he concluded that execution ought normally
to follow, and that he was further convinced
that Jesus was guilty of having professed to be
king. Jesus would then be doubly condemned
to death, in the one case by the exercise of
Pilate's power to enforce the sentence of a
Jewish court and in the second by the direct
exercise of his jurisdiction over a provincial.

What might have been the relation of this
to the Bar-Abbas incident? Here was a man
also condemned and also for rebellion. Bar-
Abbas had led an insurrection in the course
of which he had killed one or more persons
—whether Romans or provincials it does not
matter. If Jesus was a rebel, so was he, and
far worse in Roman estimation since Jesus
was not even charged with deeds of actual
violence while Bar-Abbas had been in arms.
Pilate may have been perfectly willing, even
desirous, of executing Jesus, but he must have
been far more desirous of executing Bar-Abbas.

The difficulty was that there was the established custom of pardoning a condemned criminal on the Passover feast. Pilate, anxious to
punish the armed rebel, offered the newly condemned man in his place. Bar-Abbas, how-

ever, was the popular man, as the leader of an
insurrection against a foreign master would be
likely to be. Pilate made a second attempt to
substitute Jesus for the man demanded. He
warned the crowd that the result would be the
crucifixion of Jesus. At this the mob bellowed
out its indifference to Jesus' fate.

If we contrast this inference with the one
drawn by "Mark," I think that we shall find
that it fits the facts as well. Whether it fits
it better we are certainly not entitled to say.
But it would not be a wholly indefensible position. There is even less reason than in the case
of the high priest to suppose that "Mark's"
informants had any special clue to the motives
of the actor. There is a strong reason why the
writer of a book published in Roman territory
should refrain from representing its hero as the
victim of a Roman governor. Since we have
merely the fact that Pilate preferred pardoning
Jesus to pardoning Bar-Abbas, we can con-
clude, if we choose, that it was less out of good
will toward the one than out of hostility to the
other.

Now, how does it stand with "Mark's" statements taken by themselves? They are in no
apparent contradiction with each other. There

are what may be called gaps, but those would
be inevitable. There is, however, a curious incident (14:51–52) which seems to have no connection with what precedes or what follows it.
How did it get into the story? Was there a
connection which has since been dropped out?
If so, was the omission of the connecting matter deliberate on the part of some reviser?
There is no possibility of getting these questions answered unless some fortunate accident
brings extremely early manuscripts to light—
a consummation hardly to be looked for.

"Mark" does not tell us who or what Pilate
was. Either he has condensed an older narrative or—what is more likely—he supposed that
every reader would know. Further, he does
not tell us what use the priests made of the
condemnation they had already voted. The
inscription on the cross indicates that the
charge of assuming the crown was found to be
established. That is confirmed by the jeering
of the Roman soldiers as well as of the priests.
Still, the ordinary passer-by made the other
charge the subject of his mockery—the charge
concerning the Temple which seems to have
stuck in the crop of Jesus' accusers, as we can
well suppose when we remember the enormous

importance—religious, political, and economic
—of the actual Temple structure.

Apparently, therefore, the council found
Jesus guilty on this charge also. But that is
not stated in so many words. Our text mentions only the charge of assuming messiahship.

What was the value of the testimony against
Jesus? "Mark" said the witnesses were all per-
jurers. We may believe that, unqualifiedly,
just as "Mark's" belief that they had been
suborned is equally possible. But it is also
possible that some had honestly enough mis-
understood a statement of Jesus and had reported it in the distorted form they remembered. If Jesus had been heard to prophesy the
destruction of the Temple, as "Mark" says he
did, in another place (13:1-2) excitable persons may well have believed he had said this
other thing.

The credibility of witnesses depends on a
great many things. The only clue "Mark"
gives us is the fact that the witnesses contradicted each other. That, however, is not a
proof that all lied, though it may be that
some did. Still, if in general a great many witnesses are all obviously hostile and the offenses
they charge are in many cases mutually con-

tradictory, such contradiction throws doubt upon all of them, though it does not deprive the accusation of all support.

But the claim to messiahship is admitted. Our translation does not give us the tone of the sentence. "Are you the Christ, the son of the Blessed?" it runs in our version. But "Blessed" is an ordinary title of God, whose direct appellation is avoided by Jews out of reverence. "Christ," Greek for "Messiah," further appears in Jewish sources only as "the King Messiah," the Annointed King, the promised Savior. So the priests' jeer at the crucified Jesus uses the correct and complete designation. "Christ, the King of Israel" it appears in our translation (15:32), but the proper rendering is "The Annointed King of Israel." The high priest's question therefore must have run, "Do you claim to be that Annointed King who will re-establish the Kingdom of David?" That he said the "Son of God" we may later on see reason to doubt, but if he did and Jesus answered, "I do so claim. I am the Messiah," that was the confession of a serious offense to an official who must perforce deny the claim to messiahship whether he was personally corrupt or not. And the offense confessed was ag-

gravated, if it was followed by the announcement given by "Mark" in which Jesus declared that he would appear visibly at the side
of God in an epiphany soon to take place.
To the minds of unbelievers this was a false
announcement of divine powers, and such a
false pretension was a crime.

"Mark's" statement therefore leads to the
conclusion that there was sufficient evidence
of an act which could well be construed as a
legal offense.

It is clear that "Mark" either did not know
that such an offense existed or did not believe that messianic pretensions constituted
it. Either hypothesis is possible. The only
question is whether such pretensions had ever
before been so dealt with by the court over
which the high priest presided. To that un-
fortunately we can give no answer. We have
only scanty accounts of specific cases in this
court and no account of a case like this. It
may be that the very charge itself, the accusation of religious imposture, had become obsolete. If it had, "Mark" may well have quoted
this statement on Jesus' part without the least
suspicion of its implications.

There are a few other possibilities which

ought not be ignored. Suppose the high priest
had been an intensely loyal pro-Roman. There
were Jews, especially high-placed Jews, who
were devotedly attached to the Roman government, some out of distrust of their own unruly
lower classes, some out of selfishness, some out
of dread of the surrounding tribesmen, still
others out of fear and dislike of the Parthian
Empire across the Euphrates, which was
Rome's only rival. In the same way some Indian princes are fervent supporters of the British Empire. If the high priest were one of this
class, his attitude might be determined by it.

Pilate's question and the inscription on the
cross are evidence that there was a rumor, or
an accusation, that Jesus had called himself
king—at any rate, that his followers called him
king. That rumor must have reached the high
priest as well. It is likely that in any case,
whether a determined pro-Roman or a selfish
truckler to a foreign master, he would have re-
acted to such a rumor as a Roman would. It
would make Jesus seem one more anti-Roman
agitator, and it would give an adequate reason
for enforcing in his case a charge which had in
practice become obsolete, or almost obsolete.
A man of the highest type of judicial integrity

would not have done so, but many modern instances will occur—especially in the case of
earnest conservatives—in which something
like it has seemed justifiable to men of a slightly lower judicial conscience than the highest,
who none the less remained both honest and
respectable.

Yet we must remember that it is more than
possible that the high priest was dishonest
rather than honest, and that his willingness to
find in the claim to be Messiah the confession
of guilt of a capital offense may have had as its
motive an ignoble desire to curry favor with
his superiors.

But, after all, the one impression which
"Mark's" narrative leaves is an eager wish to
prove that Jesus was completely innocent even
according to Jewish law and that there was no
credible evidence of any kind to show the contrary. In this, I think we must hold, he was
mistaken—at least as to technical guilt in accordance with an ancient code. Still, his belief
would have a large measure of justification if
such an announcement as that of Jesus had
not within recent memory been considered a
crime.

The certainty that Jesus had been unjustly

convicted is not more apparent in "Mark's" narrative than the writer's desire to place the blame on the priests, or more particularly the "chief priests," the scribes, and the elders who are mentioned several times. These in "Mark's" view certainly formed part of the Council— but not all of it. The word he uses for "Council" is the Greek *synedrion*, which is an ordinary term for a body of advisers or the governing board of a community or corporation and had already been adopted into Hebrew and Aramaic, the languages of Palestine, where it appears as "Sanhedrin." There can be scarcely any doubt that when "Mark" uses the word he means it practically as a proper name, much as we say Congress or Parliament.

Except for that, there is very little detail offered, to give either vividness or color to the narrative. Two places are mentioned, the high priest's house, which is merely indicated by the fact that Jesus is brought to him, and the official seat of the procurator. It may be stated that when our translation speaks of the "palace of the high priest" in connection with Peter, that is not a good rendering of the Greek word used, *aulē*, which means the outer court where the servants would be gathered. Jesus

was evidently in an inside room. This is also
the word used in 15:16 where it is translated
"hall." "Mark" goes on to say that the *aulē*
in Pilate's house is called the "praetorium," a
Latin word used in the Greek of that time to
describe the Roman governor's official residence. It would follow that when Pilate examined him it was not in the praetorium but in
another part of the house. It must accordingly
have been in a closed chamber which normally
would not be very large, and yet not only were
the "chief priests" present but the many witnesses and the crowd which clamored for Bar-
Abbas and for Jesus' execution. That is almost
an impossibility. It is, to be sure, not difficult
to rearrange the sequence of events so that
they might have happened in a Greek or
Roman official building at Jerusalem, but the
fact that the physical background is not quite
clear seems to show that this account does not
reproduce the report of an eyewitness. "Mark"
—if he is the writer—could not very well have
been an eyewitness, but it seems from what
has been said that even his informants were
not.

   In fact, the omission of an important fact indicates again that the scene of the trial before

Pilate is not vividly in the writer's mind. We know from Josephus and others that the procurator's official residence was not in Jerusalem at all but in Caesarea. He came into Jerusalem rarely—generally on the pilgrimage feasts—and when he did so he probably lodged in the palace of Herod the Great, which was normally unoccupied. Now, this was a tremendous structure and the name of Herod clung to it. If Jesus was examined in one of the great courts of the palace, it is strange that it is not mentioned, and that it is merely described as a praetorium, which it was only for brief periods.

Indeed if we think about it, who could have been eyewitnesses of the examination before the Sanhedrin? Mention is made only of the judges, Jesus, and the witnesses against him. Peter was outside in the *aulē*, and, as the narrative especially points out, in a state of fear for his own safety. That any disciple or friend spoke to Jesus from the moment of his incarceration in the high priest's house until his death is highly unlikely. Who told "Mark's" informant of what went on at the trial? If it was a hostile witness, it is surely not he who spoke of the contradictory statements and the

obvious perjury of himself and his associates.
We should have to assume witnesses on Jesus'
behalf of which there is no suggestion, or a
sympathetic slave, or a repentant accuser or
judge. All these sources are possible, but no
hint is given to us by "Mark" that there was
any person of this description. And he seems
to take pains to show that Peter was not present at the trial.

One possible source existed.   In "Mark"
15:42-43 we hear that "Joseph of Arimathaea,
an honorable counsellor which also waited for
the Kingdom of God," asked and received per-
mission of Pilate to bury Jesus. It is assumed
by "Mark" that Arimathea would be known
to his readers. The phrase "honorable counsellor," in Greek, *buleutēs*, can only mean
"member of the *bulē*," that is, of the national
Senate, the Sanhedrin, the body which in the
absence of Roman authority would be the
governing council of the nation. It is also said
that "he waited for the Kingdom of God."
That is, he was a convert or half-convert—at
any rate, an adherent to some extent of the
group about Jesus. There is nothing whatever
improbable in the fact that a member of the
Sanhedrin was an adherent of Jesus. But either

this reference to Joseph is a later addition to
our text or else "Mark" means us to believe
that Joseph was not present at the meeting
which condemned Jesus. To be sure, it is possible that at the meeting itself even a sympa-
thizer might have been cowed into concealing
his sympathy but one might well have expected an explanation to that effect. If Joseph
was there, he must have voted for conviction
and death, since it is expressly stated that "all"
so voted; and the "whole council" again ad-
vocated (15:1) the delivery to Pilate.

Surely, if Joseph was a member of the Sanhedrin, it is easier to believe that he was not
present than that he carried in his conscience
the sin of having voted for the death of his
master.

"Mark" does not mention the high priest's
name. He gives no explanation of Judas' treason. That the name of the high priest was well
known to his readers is possible but a little unlikely. Since this official takes so active and so
hostile a part in the proceedings against Jesus,
it seems strange that the writer should have
failed to hold his name up to obloquy, if he
knew it. He does so in the case of Judas. Perhaps, after all, he did not know the name,

which, in any case, is not essential to his narrative.

In fact, it is noteworthy that even the part of Judas is not emphasized. Without any preliminaries Judas is stated to have offered to betray Jesus and to have done so. Nothing further is said about him, and except for the fact that he was one of the twelve disciples, he never had been mentioned before. But the plot on the part of the "chief priests" is referred to at the very beginning. Judas' treason, "Mark" wishes to show, merely gave them the opportunity they had been seeking. But, just as Judas is not the object of "Mark's" animosity, so it is not even the unnamed high priest who is in the last analysis responsible for the death of Jesus. That responsibility is really borne by the group he calls the "chief priests," a term which in Greek is exactly the same as that which is used for the "high priest." It is they —not the high priest—who suborn the witnesses, they who encourage the multitude to repeat their cry for Bar-Abbas, they who taunt Jesus with his messiahship. In fact, the high priest proper appears only at the trial and neither in the plot which led to the trial nor in the examination before Pilate and in the Bar-

Abbas incident which led to the execution. Apparently the "chief priests" constitute a definite body, distinct from the scribes, the elders, and the rest of the Council (the Sanhedrin).

Who they are "Mark" evidently supposed his readers would know. Or else, if the Gospel is later than we ordinarily suppose, the writer had a vague group of ecclesiastical officials in mind without much concern for their correct designation or their position in the community. Whether there was such a body in the formal sense and whoever they were "Mark" thinks of them as Jesus' enemies, almost his sole enemies. Pilate surely, Judas, even the high priest, if he is not of their number, are little more than means by which they wreak their spite on Jesus.

Slight as "Mark's" details are, on either the physical or the institutional side, he makes one thing clear. It was the action of the ecclesiastical authorities which resulted in Jesus' arrest and conviction, and there are no other civil authorities of the Jews at all. It is not merely that he omits to speak of them. It seems clear enough from his narrative that the Sanhedrin and the chief priests represented the only form of national government that existed. "Mark" attacks the justice of the trial but not the right of the court to try Jesus. In modern legal parlance, he does question the jurisdiction of the Sanhedrin.

Again we may draw another obvious inference. The chief priests were eager to put Jesus to death. The Sanhedrin condemned him to death. Why was he not executed at once? There is no possible inference except that the Sanhedrin and the high priest had no power to carry out a capital sentence.

And the fifteenth chapter adds a new implication. Jesus does not appeal to the procurator. Yet he gets, as a matter of course, what he would have had had he appealed. The chief priests present him bound as a man already condemned by the national court to the Roman representative, and they bring witnesses. If these witnesses repeat what had been said before the Sanhedrin, the proceedings are in effect a review of the trial. But, as has been said, that does not seem to have been the legal relation of the two courts. Before any accusations were made by the chief priests, Pilate asked Jesus about the title of king. Jesus uses words which may have seemed like an evasion but he certainly does not admit having assumed the title. It may be then that the witnesses testify to this fact and that the trial before Pilate relates only to it.

We have therefore, in "Mark's" account, statements from which we can infer with relative certainty the limitations on the Sanhedrin's and the high priest's power and from which we can further infer that the determining decision as to execution rested with the procurator. We can however not be sure whether he would usually review the case completely and affirm or disapprove the sentence or whether he would accept the verdict of the Sanhedrin as final, and merely make additional investigations in order to decide how he should exercise his discretion.

We may finally infer that the relation of governor and governed in "Mark's" account implied a strong desire on the part of the former not to exasperate the latter. The customary pardon at the feast, the disinclination to resist their wishes too much, show that Roman authority in this section felt strongly the need of a certain measure of popular support.

We may sum up the testimony of "Mark" by saying the following: It is incomplete; it is not wholly clear and in some details obviously con-

fused. "Mark" does not indicate the source of
his evidence for the Sanhedrin trial, and without such indication, we are reduced to rather
unlikely conjectures about that source. But in
essentials "Mark" is convinced and means to
convince us that there was no crime, by Jewish
law or by any law, of which Jesus was guilty,
that his conviction was obtained by perjury,
that only a prejudiced court would have condemned him, and that the Roman procurator
would have been glad to pardon him.

CHAPTER II

MATTHEW

26: 1. And it came to pass, when Jesus had finished all these sayings, he said unto his disciples,

2. Ye know that after two days is the feast of the passover, and the Son of man is betrayed to be crucified.

3. Then assembled together the chief priests, and the scribes, and the elders of the people, unto the palace of the high priest, who was called Caiaphas,

4. And consulted that they might take Jesus by subtilty, and kill him.

5. But they said, Not on the feast-day, lest there be an uproar among the people.

14. Then one of the twelve, called Judas Iscariot, went unto the chief priests,

15. And said unto them, What will ye give me, and I will deliver him unto you? And they covenanted with him for thirty pieces of silver.

16. And from that time he sought opportunity to betray him.

47. And while he yet spake, lo, Judas, one of the twelve, came, and with him a great multitude with swords and staves, from the chief priests and elders of the people.

48. Now he betrayed him, gave them a sign, saying, Whomsoever I shall kiss, that same is he; hold him fast.

49. And forthwith he came to Jesus, and said, Hail Master; and kissed him.

50. And Jesus said unto him, Friend, wherefore art thou come? Then came they, and laid hands on Jesus, and took him.

51. And behold, one of them which were with Jesus, stretched out his hand, and drew his sword, and struck a servant of the high priest, and smote off his ear.

52. Then said Jesus unto him, Put up again thy sword into his place: for all they that take the sword, shall perish with the sword.

53. Thinkest thou that I cannot now pray to my Father, and he shall presently give me more than twelve legions of angels?

54. But how then shall the scriptures be fulfilled, that thus it must be?

55. In that same hour said Jesus to the multitudes, Are ye come out as against a thief with swords and staves for to take me? I sat daily with you teaching in the temple, and ye laid no hold on me.

56. But all this was done, that the scriptures of the prophets might be fulfilled. Then all the disciples forsook him, and fled.

57. And they that had laid hold on Jesus, led him away to Caiaphas the high priest, where the scribes and the elders were assembled.

58. But Peter followed him afar off, unto the high priest's palace, and went in, and sat with the servants to see the end.

59. Now the chief priests, and elders, and all the council, sought false witness against Jesus, to put him to death;

60. But found none: yea, though many false witnesses came, yet found they none. At the last came two false witnesses,

61. And said, This fellow said, I am able to destroy the temple of God, and to build it in three days.

62. And the 'high priest arose, and said unto him, Answerest thou nothing? what is it which these witness against thee?

63. But Jesus held his peace. And the high priest answered and said unto him, I adjure thee by the living God, that thou tell us whether thou be the Christ the Son of God.

64. Jesus saith unto him, Thou hast said: nevertheless, I say unto you, Hereafter shall ye see the Son of man sitting on the right hand of power, and coming in the clouds of heaven.

65. Then the high priest rent his clothes, saying, He hath spoken blasphemy; what further need have we of witnesses? behold now ye have heard his blasphemy.

66. What think ye? They answered and said, He is guilty of death.

67. Then did they spit in his face, and buffeted him; and others smote him with the palms of their hands.

68. Saying, Prophesy unto us, thou Christ, Who is he that smote thee?

27: 1. When the morning was come, all the chief priests and elders of the people took counsel against Jesus to put him to death.

2. And when they had bound him, they led him away, and delivered him to Pontius Pilate the governor.

3. Then Judas, which has betrayed him, when he saw that he was condemned, repented himself, and brought again the thirty pieces of silver to the chief priests and elders.

4. Saying, I have sinned in that I have betrayed the innocent blood. And they said, What is that to us? see thou to that.

5. And he cast down the pieces of silver in the temple, and departed, and went and hanged himself.

6. And the chief priests took the silver pieces, and said, It is not lawful for to put them into the treasury, because it is the price of blood.

7. And they took counsel, and bought with them the potter's field, to bury strangers in.

8. Wherefore that field was called, The field of blood, unto this day.

9. Then was fulfilled that which was spoken by Jeremy the prophet, saying, And they took the thirty pieces of silver, the price of him that was valued, whom they of the children of Israel did value;

10. And gave them for the potter's field, as the Lord appointed me.

11. And Jesus stood before the governor: and the governor asked him, saying, Art thou the King of the Jews? And Jesus said unto him, Thou sayest.

12. And when he was accused of the chief priests and elders, he answered nothing.

13. Then saith Pilate unto him, Hearest thou not how many things they witness against thee?

14. And he answered him to never a word: insomuch that the governor marvelled greatly.

15. Now at that feast, the governor was wont to release unto the people a prisoner, whom they would.

16. And they had then a notable prisoner called Barabbas.

17. Therefore, when they were gathered together, Pilate said unto them, Whom will ye that I release unto you? Barabbas, or Jesus, which is called Christ?

18. For he knew that for envy they had delivered him.

19. When he was set down on the judgment-seat, his wife said unto him, saying, Have thou nothing to do with that just man: for I have suffered many things this day in a dream, because of him.

20. But the chief priests and elders persuaded the multitude that they should ask Barabbas, and destroy Jesus.

21. The governor answered and said unto them,
Whether of the twain will ye that I release unto
you? They said, Barabbas.

22. Pilate saith unto them, What shall I do then
with Jesus, which is called Christ? They all say
unto him, Let him be crucified.

23. And the governor said, Why, what evil hath he
done? But they cried out the more, saying, Let
him be crucified.

24. When Pilate saw that he could prevail nothing,
but that rather a tumult was made, he took
water, and washed his hands before the multitude, saying, I am innocent of the blood of this
just person: see ye to it.

25. Then answered all the people, and said, His
blood be on us, and on our children.

26. Then released he Barabbas unto them: and
when he had scourged Jesus, he delivered him
to be crucified.

27. Then the soldiers of the governor took Jesus into
the common hall, and gathered unto him the
whole band of soldiers.

28. And they stripped him, and put on him a scarlet
robe.

29. And when they had platted a crown of thorns,
they put it upon his head, and a reed in his right
hand: and they bowed the knee before him, and
mocked him, saying Hail, King of the Jews!

30. And they spit upon him, and took the reed, and
smote him on the head.

31. And after that they had mocked him, they took

the robe off from him, and put his own raiment on him, and led him away to crucify him.

32. And as they came out, they found a man of Cyrene, Simon by name: him they compelled to bear his cross.

33. And when they were come unto a place called Golgotha, that is to say, A place of a skull,

34. They gave him vinegar to drink, mingled with gall: and when he had tasted thereof, he would not drink.

35. And they crucified him, and parted his garments, casting lots: that it might be fulfilled which was spoken by the prophet: They parted my garments among them, and upon my vesture did they cast lots.

36. And sitting down, they watched him there:

37. And set up over his head his accusation written, THIS IS JESUS THE KING OF THE JEWS.

38. Then were there two thieves crucified with him: one on the right hand, and another on the left.

39. And they that passed by, reviled him, wagging their heads,

40. And saying, Thou that destroyest the temple, and buildest it in three days, save thyself. If thou be the Son of God, come down from the cross.

41. Likewise also the chief priests mocking him, with the scribes and elders, said,

42. He saved others; himself he cannot save. If he be the King of Israel, let him now come down from the cross, and we will believe him.

43. He trusteth in God; let him deliver him now if
he will have him: for he said, I am the Son of
God.

44. The thieves also which were crucified with him,
cast the same in his teeth.

This is the story as it is told in the book we
know as the Gospel of St. Matthew, or, more
precisely, as the Gospel according to St. Matthew. As in the case of "Mark" we must have
some tentative theory about its authorship.
That is especially necessary here, more necessary than in the case of "Mark." The author
of "Mark" even by ancient tradition was not a
direct witness of the scenes he depicts. He re-
lied on informants, and while it would be important to know whether the informants spoke
at first hand, it is not essential We might accept unqualifiedly the tradition which names
the writer as John, surnamed Marcus, the son
of Mary and the younger friend of the apostle
Peter, without either abandoning a critical
attitude or rejecting the whole account as an
invention.

But in the case of "Matthew," the problem
is a much more serious one. "Matthew," like
John Mark, was a real person, and, unlike
"Mark," he was the follower and close asso-

ciate of Jesus. He played a prominent part among his fellow-disciples. If "Matthew" is the author whose work is before us, he ought to be considered an eyewitness of many of the things he describes. He must have been present at the arrest and, if he was, he must have been one of those who "forsook him and fled." He cannot have been a witness of the trial before the Sanhedrin, any more than "Mark's" informant. But he may well from a distance have seen the examination before Pilate and Crucifixion. He must have known Judas and been able to judge his character. He may have seen Judas after Jesus' death. If we take Matthew to be the author, we must either accept his statements as to the things he witnesses as true, or charge him with a dishonesty for which there is no warrant.

And yet, of the things mentioned, there are after all very few about which we can say that he must necessarily have witnessed them. The historical Matthew may have been present at the trial before Pilate or at the Crucifixion, but it does not follow that he was. According to his own account he fled at the arrest. He may have remained in hiding for several days. If it was more than three days, even Jesus' body, according to the gospel, had disappeared from its tomb. As to these things, then, "Matthew's" account would be only to this degree better than "Mark's" that he had it from people who had recently seen it and not, as in the case of "Mark," from people who had seen the events long ago.

And this circumstance might make it less valuable rather than more. Suppose it is really the story of Jesus' intimate associate and follower which we have, and suppose, further, that he learned the details of the examination before Pilate and of the Crucifixion shortly after the event, from someone who had with his own eyes seen those dreadful things. What can we think the emotional state to have been of one who had been so near to the person of Jesus? The excitement of the arrest, the panic of the flight, the terror of the following days of hiding, the indignation at the fate of a master he believed to be nothing less than divine, present a condition of mind which is not the best for accurate testimony. And the recollection of all these things could hardly have been improved as time went on, as the band of followers grew into an organized corporation, as rivalries arose and conflicts became established, and as the conviction of having been associated with an incarnate God, soon to reappear again with the thunders of the Last Day, became a cardinal doctrine of faith. All this would make it necessary to scrutinize his testimony on every point where emotion or religious zeal could possibly color it.

This is all on the assumption that we have Matthew's narrative. Let us ask ourselves not what reason there is to question it, but what reason there is to believe it. Nowhere in the course of the book is the author's name stated or indicated. That Matthew wrote the gospel of that name is a tradition, an old one, to be sure, but still several centuries later than the time of Matthew. Indeed, as far as these particular chapters are concerned, the first direct statement that they are by Matthew is not older than our first Bible manuscript, and that is about A.D. 375. Not only does the writer nowhere name himself or indicate who he is, but he nowhere suggests that he is writing as a witness. He does not distinguish between the arrest which he must have seen, the trial before Pilate which he may have seen, and the trial before the Sanhedrin which he can scarcely have seen. They are all told in the same neutral third person. That is in the main in the ancient style, as can be seen in Caesar's *Commentaries*, but Caesar's suppressions of his position as the writer of his history seem to have been deliberate and the first person occasionally crops out. In the case of other books which are more directly of the same general type as the gospel—books like the *Memorabilia* of Socrates, written by his pupil Xenophon— the intrusion of the writer is fairly common. If we recall that Matthew cannot have been a trained rhetorician, as Caesar and, to a certain extent, Xenophon were, but a provincial belonging to a rude and ill-famed calling, we should certainly expect a clearer indication of the fact that the writer of the story was also one of the actors in it.

All this does not prove that Matthew did not write the gospel which bears his name, but it deprives us of any good evidence that he did, and it therefore makes the discussion of his credibility as an eyewitness less necessary. In fact, we must assume in the absence of proof that, as in the case of "Mark," this story is a story written down by one who was not an eyewitness but got his account at second or third or fourth hand, and we cannot be quite sure that even his ultimate source was an eye-witness.

What are the new elements which "Matthew" introduces?

First of all he gives us names where "Mark" omits them. He too speaks of "chief priests" and their obvious head, the "high priest," and uses for both the Greek *archiereus*, but he gives the high priest's name not casually but as though he were adding an elucidating comment—"the palace of the High Priest, who was called Caiaphas" (26:3). Similarly of the Roman governor it is said (27:2), "and delivered him to Pontius Pilate the governor." The name is given more fully than in "Mark"—not quite completely, however—and we are told who he was. He was the "governor." The Greek is *hegemon*, properly a military title meaning "leader," and not the exact equivalent of Pilate's actual title of "procurator." That would in Greek have been *epitropos*, as hundreds of inscriptions and papyri and texts tell us. *Hegemon* was in later times frequently used as the general word for "official" or even "governor," but we are not sure it was so used in the time of Jesus or in the period immediately after. In any case, "Matthew" felt he

could not take for granted that his hearers
would know who Pilate was, as "Mark" must
have felt. And he thought that the identity of
the high priest was important and so gave his
name.

In one thing "Matthew" is less explicit.
"Mark" knew who Bar-Abbas was and told
us. He was an insurgent chief, an open rebel
with blood on his hands. And "Mark" makes
a point of the fact that he was saved, whereas
Jesus, who had done no violence and against
whom no treason had been proved, was killed.

To "Matthew," Bar-Abbas was merely a
"notable prisoner." It really made no difference who or what he was as far as "Matthew"
is concerned. If we had no other source, we
might have guessed that Bar-Abbas was an innocent and harmless victim of oppression. To
prefer anyone to Jesus was in "Matthew's"
eyes the great sin, and to "Matthew's" readers,
who already believed Jesus to be "very God,"
it could not seem otherwise.

As to the course of events, there are differences to which we may be compelled to attach
significance. The scribes and the high priest
take part in the plot to put Jesus to death. In
"Mark" the high priest is not mentioned.

Again we meet the uncertainty as to whether the elders who were with the chief priests and scribes in Caiaphas' house were the whole Council (Sanhedrin) or part of it. But in "Matthew" the scribes and elders all join in binding Jesus and taking him to Pilate. In "Mark" it is only the chief priests. In "Mark" the mob clamors for Bar-Abbas of its own accord at first. In "Matthew" the plan to ask for Bar-Abbas is from the beginning a plan of the chief priests and elders. The story is interrupted in "Matthew" by the curious intrusion of the incident concerning Pilate's wife (27:19), which seems to be out of place here and to belong rather before verse 11, or after verse 3. But the change in the part played by the priests is obviously intentional. Similarly, the mockers are not merely the chief priests and scribes as in "Mark," but the chief priests, scribes, and elders, and they use in mockery the words "He said, I am the Son of God." "Mark's" scoffers have in mind mainly the claim to be the Messiah, which in "Mark" appears in its technically correct Jewish form, the "Anjointed King of Israel." Above all, the formal acceptance of responsibility by the mob for themselves and their children is an announcement by the writer of his attitude in the matter. This incident, which is not in "Mark" at all, makes unmistakable what "Matthew" wishes his readers to believe on the question of who were principally guilty of Jesus' death.

We may infer that "Matthew" is concerned to make the Jewish participation in the death of Jesus somewhat greater by describing all the Jewish authorities—chief priests, scribes, elders—as taking an active part in all its stages.

And just as the part of the Jews is increased, so the Roman part is lessened. Pilate does not merely twice propose Jesus instead of Bar-Abbas as the recipient of the customary pardon, but he officially and solemnly clears himself of the guilt of his death by washing his hands, while the multitude willingly accepts responsibility for themselves and their children. This is somewhat inconsistent with the flogging and with the brutality of the Roman soldiers which immediately follows, but the inconsistency is not so important in itself as the indication it furnishes of "Matthew's" own point of view. The Jewish authorities, all of them, and the people as far as they are represented by the mob about the praetorium are held up to the execration of his readers. The Roman authority—the person representing the Roman state—is to be cleared as far as possible. We may draw whatever inferences we like as to his reasons for accentuating the part of the former and lightening the part of the latter. The essential thing is that he obviously seeks to do so.

There is a difficulty in his attempt. "Matthew" realizes that the governor's power was quite extensive enough to pardon both Bar-Abbas and Jesus. The decision in the last analysis is his alone. In "Mark" he chooses to execute Jesus and pardon Bar-Abbas, because he was "willing to content the people." That involves an assumption of responsibility, even if the request comes from the crowd. But in "Matthew's" account Pilate ordered the execution for fear of a riot (27:24)—"when Pilate saw he could prevail nothing, but that rather a tumult was made." To give occasion to a disturbance, especially in so unruly a province, was a dangerous thing for Pilate and for Rome. The readers of "Matthew" would take it as a proof that Pilate had yielded to pressure, that his hand was forced, and this, together with the ceremonial washing of the hands, would absolve him from most of the responsibility. The incident of "Pilate's wife"—if it is not a much later addition—has a similar effect. All the Roman personages, except the soldiers, seek to save Jesus and testify to his innocence. They call him"this just man," *dikaios*, which in this connection means "guiltless."

But directly after we have the identical words which were used by "Mark": "When he had scourged Jesus, he delivered him up to be crucified." The Greek indicates, just as the English version shows, that the scourging was done under the immediate direction of the procurator, before Jesus was surrendered to the executioner. That fits in well enough with "Mark," but hardly with "Matthew." Then again the inscription of the accusation is as before, "This is the King of the Jews." That is precisely what Pilate presented to Jesus as the accusation against him. It was no part of the charges made in the Sanhedrin, and it would not have been a crime at Jewish law to make such a claim. Apparently even in "Matthew's" account Pilate after all must have found Jesus guilty of an attempt at rebellion.

Later commentators have suggested that Pilate is hypocritical throughout, that he made

no real effort to save him and had no desire to
do so, but merely pretended to do it, out of
some vague intimation of Jesus' divine character. There is not a touch of evidence for that
in anything "Matthew" says, and therefore no
reason whatever for supposing it.

In the Sanhedrin trial there are two noteworthy differences between "Mark" and "Matthew." In "Matthew" after several futile efforts to find witnesses two witnesses appear to
testify to the alleged statement of Jesus that
he could destroy the Temple and rebuild it.
"Mark" merely states that there were several.
It was important to indicate that there were
more than one, since if Jesus had been condemned on the testimony of only one witness
the proceedings would have been flagrantly
and openly illegal. It was not only a matter
of statute but of strong popular feeling that no
man might be condemned by the mouth of one
witness. But "Matthew" takes pains to say
that the number was the smallest possible that
could have led to a conviction.

Besides this one fact, "Matthew," who ordinarily gives more details than "Mark," says
nothing whatever about the witnesses except
that they were false. We have seen that neither

he nor "Mark" can have been present at the
trial, but "Mark" takes pains to offer specific
proof that they were false by explaining that
they contradicted each other. That, as has
been said, is not quite enough, but it undoubtedly qualifies the value of the testimony con-
siderably and before a modern jury as before
an ancient judge might justify the rejection of
all the witnesses. "Mark" is evidently concerned to offer convincing proof of the injustice of the conviction of Jesus.

"Matthew," however, seems to care less for
that. Whether the witnesses contradicted each
other or not, he is satisfied that they lied. The
legality of the proceedings against Jesus must
have seemed to "Matthew" somewhat irrelevant. He evidently firmly believes that Jesus
was Messiah and the Son of God, and he cannot very well entertain the notion that the assumption of these titles could possibly constitute a crime in any system of law. However,
he is sufficiently conscious of the fact that these
very designations were made the subject of the
charges against Jesus, so that he does not represent Jesus as unequivocally admitting them.
The high priest asks Jesus, "Art thou the
Messiah?" Pilate asks, "Art thou the King of

the Jews?" To both questions Jesus answers,
"Thou hast said it." "Mark" makes a difference in the answers. Jesus in "Mark's" account unqualifiedly claims messiahship before
the Sanhedrin and uses the other phrase only
before Pilate. If it is too much to say that the
expression "Thou sayest it" is an evasion, it is
certainly less than an unconditional admission.
"Mark" makes the high priest's statement that
Jesus had uttered a blasphemy intelligible. It
is less intelligible in "Matthew's" account.

That "Matthew" is less troubled than
"Mark" about the legality of the procedure is
confirmed by another observation. "Mark"
ends the Sanhedrin trial with the single statement (14:64): "And they all condemned him
to be guilty of death." "Matthew" puts it in
dialogue form (26:66): "They answered and
said 'He is guilty of death'" (27:1). In
"Mark" the condemnation is treated as final
and Jesus is bound and delivered to the Roman
governor (13:1). Apparently "Mark" has in
mind the fact that in the normal course of
events Pilate would carry out the sentence.
There is no indication in either narrative that
the priests anticipated Pilate's attitude on the
Bar-Abbas incident. It would not have been

impossible for them to have done so, but there is no suggestion to that effect. "Mark," in other words, while deeply stirred about the injustice of Jesus' conviction, knows the things which gave it an air of legality and attempts to meet them specifically, or rather wishes to show their triviality as compared with the patent innocence of Jesus of any real crime. "Matthew" seems to have less clearly in mind what the priestly enemies of Jesus would have deemed a valid conviction.

In the naming of the high priest and the fuller designation of Pilate we may see a slight attempt to give vividness and color to the narrative. The difference in the condemnation seems to be a case in point—and this, we must recall again and again—is a matter about which direct evidence was almost impossible. "Matthew" makes the taunt to Jesus, "Prophesy unto us, thou Christ, who is he that smote thee," the occasion of cruel jesting (27:67) in a cruder form than that in which "Mark" reports it. But the most effectively dramatic incident is the story of Judas' repentance, a story wholly absent from "Mark."

The fact that "Mark" does not mention it does not mean that it is an invention of "Matthew's" or of anybody's. In itself the incident is rather probable than not. Such agonies of remorse on the part of a traitor are extremely common, especially if the treason was caused by a sudden outburst of violent resentment. We do not know that this was so in the case of Judas, but it might have been. And even if the motive was purely sordid, the imagination that could contemplate the treason and the profit might have been wholly unequal to the task of envisaging the actual horror of seeing his former master on the cross, and when this became realized there was an inevitable re-action.

But if the story of the repentance is quite probable in itself, the manner in which it is told makes it rather improbable. There is no sufficient reason for the chief priest's refusal to pick the money up, even if it was blood-money. They were not required to use it for sacred purposes, and to suppose that they had any personal feeling in regard to it would imply compunctions about Jesus' death, which in the position "Matthew" gives the story somewhat contradicts the subsequent action of the priests.

In fact, the way in which the story is told

makes it strikingly like similar stories told in almost all literature. It seems to be introduced to explain the name Aceldama, which was the designation of the strangers' burial place at Jerusalem, and which might mean "Field of Blood." At any rate, stories like it, explaining a current and somewhat striking term, are the commonest forms of legends.

We may note that in this account "Matthew" contradicts a story which is found in another book of the New Testament, the Acts of the Apostles (1:19). Peter is there reported as describing Judas' death. In this account Judas used his money to buy a field and was there killed by what apparently is described as a fatal accident, an accident giving the field its name. Undoubtedly such an accident would seem to be a divine judgment. The Acts say nothing of the fact that this was the public burying ground or that the latter included Aceldama.

The story as "Matthew" gives it implies that until the death of Judas there was no public or strangers' burying ground near Jerusalem. This however is excessively unlikely. All our ancient Jewish sources for this period—that is, Josephus, Philo, and the Talmud—speak of the duty of burying the unclaimed dead as one of the most ancient and obligatory of Israelitish forms of charity, in every case referring its institution to Moses. It is scarcely conceivable that any ancient city could have existed without some provision for this purpose.

One might wonder why the priests did not use Judas as a witness as well as a stool pigeon. He would have been invaluable. If his effrontery enabled him to greet Jesus when he came from his last lodging, it should have been equal to testifying, especially since the literal truth would have given the high priest a legal justification for the arrest. Of course, there is a difference in the two acts, and Judas' boldness may have oozed out quickly. Yet, after all, the elapsed time is incredibly short. Jesus was arrested in the evening and arraigned before the high priest almost at once.

Whether all this really happened so or not, it is quite clear that Judas bore no testimony against Jesus. This is a case in which omission to state a fact is almost certain proof of its non-existence as far as the narrator was concerned. No reason can be imagined for failing to mention such testimony of Judas, if it had taken place. We must leave the matter there without any satisfactory reason as to why Caiaphas made no attempt to utilize Judas' services further than he did.

The difficulty in "Mark" about the position of Joseph of Arimathea disappears in "Matthew's" account. "Matthew" also implies that the Council of Elders condemned Jesus unanimously although he does not use the words "all" or "the whole." But in his reference to Joseph (27:57) there is no mention of his rank. He is merely a "rich man of Arimathea, named Joseph, who also himself was Jesus' disciple." It is highly likely that "Matthew" deliberately discarded the term "counselor," whether he found it in a written book which he was using, or knew of it by tradition for the reason that it implied Joseph's condemnation of Jesus. The implication could scarcely have helped occurring to later retellers of the story, even if in the earlier accounts it may have passed unnoticed.

There are a few small matters which are difficult—though not impossible—to reconcile in the accounts of both "Mark" and "Matthew." Jesus was, like Bar-Abbas, a "notable person," according to both gospels, with no inconsiderble popularity. It was so plainly the case that the chief priests dared not arrest him at once while the city was crowded for the first day of the Passover. Pilate speaks of him as a man well known. Jesus himself states that he had constantly been in the public view in and around the Temple. And yet the chief priests do not know him by sight and can identify him only with the help of Judas. That is certainly a little strange.

Another difference between "Mark" and "Matthew" is that in the latter's account Jesus at the Supper does not merely speak in general of a traitor in their midst, but specifically names Judas (26:25). "Matthew" apparently does not wish it to be said that Jesus, whose divine character is far more stressed than it is in "Mark," did not know precisely who the traitor was. In case Judas was so named, the subsequent arrest is rendered a little more difficult. Judas must have been somewhat in advance of his escort when he greeted Jesus. Why was he allowed to approach so near? One at least of the disciples (26:51)—he is not named—drew his sword and attacked the soldiers. One should suppose that this man would be roused to something like frenzy at the approach of a traitor denounced by name by the Master. Yet Judas is suffered to kiss him.

"Matthew" puts in Jesus' mouth the statement that if he chose he might have called more than twelve legions of angels to his aid (26:53). If that was publicly made, that is, in the hearing of those who made the arrest—and it seems to have been—the priests would have had evidence of "false prophecy" as patent as the statement about the Temple, since it was an assertion of miraculous power. To "Matthew" and his readers it was the literal truth. It would not have seemed so to Jesus' opponents.

"Mark" says nothing of this. It does not sound like a real tradition.

In their accounts of the Passion, "Matthew" and "Mark" bear the same relation to each other as scholars have found them to bear in the whole gospel narrative. "Matthew" is longer and has more details. He has several which are complete incidents in themselves and could easily be completely removed without the least interruption of the story. One of them—the incident of Pilate's wife—does not seem to have been very skilfully inserted.

While he adds details to "Mark's" narrative,

he omits none except the unrelated and, in its present form, irrational, detail (Mark 14:51–52) —of the young man who was stripped naked. He makes minute changes in "Mark's" story and nearly every change is a slight rationalization, that is, a change that relieves the account of a little difficulty.

If we met these facts in books that had no claim to our reverence, we should normally draw the inference that one account presupposes the other, that "Matthew" had "Mark" before him and sought to some extent to supplement and correct his account. And this is just the inference which biblical scholars have drawn. Of course, if we could be quite sure of it, that would completely dispose of the supposed authorship of "Matthew," but, as we have seen, there is no real evidence for that authorship in any case.

We cannot say that in this part of the gospel, the additions which "Matthew" gives have the air of historical material. They have all the look of legends, and the story of Judas' repentance, besides being of a type familiar in legends, involves contradictions with other accounts in both the New Testament and outside of it.

As to the changes which he makes, they are evidently intended to clarify the narrative, but in some cases they seem rather to confuse it. What they do indicate, however, may, I think, be fairly called an effort to accentuate the Jewish responsibility for the death of Jesus. Something of that is already apparent in "Mark." In "Matthew" it is emphasized. It would be a quite natural attitude to take by those who spoke for the Christian communities when the separation from the Jewish congregations was already an established fact. Christian apologetes of the second century were prone to stress their good citizenship as contrasted with the rebellious Jews. It was an important element to make it clear that Jesus' execution was in no real sense a Roman act. The apocryphal books go even farther in this respect and end by making Pilate a convert. Similarly in the writings of the Samaritans who suffered constant bloody suppressions by Roman authorities, it is the Jews and not the Romans who are described as the oppressors.

We must keep this tendency in mind in considering "Matthew," especially in those details in which he has changed "Mark's" story or added to it.

CHAPTER III

LUKE

22: 1. Now the feast of unleavened bread drew nigh,
which is called the Passover.
2. And the chief priests and scribes sought how
they might kill him: for they feared the people.
3. Then entered Satan into Judas surnamed Iscariot, being of the number of the twelve.
4. And he went his way, and communed with the
chief priests and captains, how he might betray
him unto them.
5. And they were glad, and covenanted to give him
money.
6. And he promised, and sought opportunity to betray him unto them in the absence of the multitude.

21. But behold, the hand of him that betrayeth me
is with me on the table.
22. And truly the Son of man goeth as it was determined: but woe unto that man by whom he
is betrayed!
23. And they began to inquire among themselves,
which of them it was that should do this thing.

47. And while he yet spake, behold a multitude,
and he that was called Judas, one of the twelve,

went before them, and drew near unto Jesus to kiss him.

48. But Jesus said unto him, Judas, betrayest thou the Son of man with a kiss?

49. When they which were about him saw what would follow, they said unto him, Lord, shall we smite with the sword?

50. And one of them smote the servant of the high priest, and cut off his right ear.

51. And Jesus answered and said, Suffer ye thus far. And he touched his ear, and healed him.

52. Then Jesus said unto the chief priests, and captains of the temple, and the elders which were come to him, Be ye come out as against a thief, with swords and staves?

53. When I was daily with you in the temple, ye stretched forth no hands against me: but this is your hour, and the power of darkness.

54. Then took they him, and led him, and brought him into the high priest's house. And Peter followed afar off.

55. And when they had kindled a fire in the midst of the hall, and were set down together, Peter sat down among them.

56. But a certain maid beheld him as he sat by the fire, and earnestly looked upon him and said, This man was also with him.

57. And he denied him, saying, Woman, I know him not.

58. And after a little while another saw him, and said, Thou art also of them. And Peter said, Man, I am not.

59. And about the space of one hour after, another confidently affirmed, saying, Of a truth this fellow also was with him; for he is a Galilean.

60. And Peter said, Man, I know not what thou sayest. And immediately, while he yet spake, the cock crew.

61. And the Lord turned, and looked upon Peter. And Peter remembered the word of the Lord, how he had said unto him, Before the cock crow, thou shalt deny me thrice.

62. And Peter went out and wept bitterly.

63. And the men that held Jesus, mocked him, and smote him.

64. And when they had blindfolded him, they struck him on the face, and asked him, saying, Prophesy, who is it that smote thee?

65. And many other things blasphemously spake they against him.

66. And as soon as it was day, the elders of the people, and the chief priests, and the scribes came together, and led him into their council, saying,

67. Art thou the Christ? tell us. And he said unto them, If I tell you, ye will not believe.

68. And if I also ask you, ye will not answer me, nor let me go.

69. Hereafter shall the Son of man sit on the right hand of the power of God.

70. Then said they all, Art thou then the Son of God? And he said unto them, Ye say that I am.

71. And they said, What need we any further witness? for we ourselves have heard of his own mouth.

23: 1. And the whole multitude of them arose, and led him unto Pilate.

2. And they began to accuse him, saying, We found this fellow perverting the nation, and forbidding to give tribute to Cesar, saying, that he himself is Christ, a King.

3. And Pilate asked him, saying, Art thou the King of the Jews? And he answered him and said, Thou sayest it.

4. Then said Pilate to the chief priests, and to the people, I find no fault in this man.

5. And they were the more fierce, saying, He stirreth up the people, teaching throughout all Jewry, beginning from Galilee to this place.

6. When Pilate heard of Galilee, he asked whether the man were a Galilean.

7. And as soon as he knew that he belonged unto Herod's jurisdiction, he sent him to Herod, who himself was at Jerusalem at that time.

8. And when Herod saw Jesus, he was exceeding glad: for he was desirous to see him of a long season, because he had heard many things of him: and he hoped to have seen some miracle done by him.

9. Then he questioned with him in many words; but he answered him nothing.

10. And the chief priests and scribes stood and vehemently accused him.

11. And Herod with his men of war set him at nought, and mocked him, and arrayed him in a gorgeous robe, and sent him again to Pilate.

12. And the same day Pilate and Herod were made friends together; for before they were at enmity between themselves.

13. And Pilate, when he had called together the chief priests, and the rulers, and the people.

14. Said unto them, Ye have brought this man unto me, as one that perverteth the people: and behold, I, having examined him before you, have found no fault in this man, touching those things whereof ye accuse him;

15. No, nor yet Herod: for I sent you to him; and lo, nothing worthy of death is done unto him:

16. I will therefore chastise him, and release him.

17. (For of necessity he must release one unto them at the feast.)

18. And they cried out all at once, saying, Away with this man, and release unto us Barabbas:

19. (Who, for a certain sedition made in the city, and for murder, was cast into prison.)

20. Pilate therefore, willing to release Jesus, spake again to them.

21. But they cried, saying, Crucify him, crucify him.

22. And he said unto them the third time, Why, what evil hath he done? I have found no cause of death in him; I will therefore chastise him, and let him go.

23. And they were instant with loud voices, requiring that he might be crucified: and the voices of them and of the chief priests prevailed.

24. And Pilate gave sentence that it should be as they required.

25. And he released unto them him that for sedition and murder was cast into prison, whom they had desired; but he delivered Jesus to their will.

26. And as they led him away, they laid hold upon one Simon a Cyrenian, coming out of the country, and on him they laid the cross, that he might bear it after Jesus.

27. And there followed him a great company of people, and of women, which also bewailed and lamented him.

28. But Jesus turning unto them, said, Daughters of Jerusalem, weep not for me, but weep for yourselves, and for your children.

29. For behold, the days are coming, in the which they shall say, Blessed are the barren, and the wombs that never bare, and the paps which never gave suck.

30. Then shall they begin to say to the mountains, Fall on us; and to the hills, Cover us.

31. For if they do these things in a green tree, what shall be done in the dry?

32. And there were also two others, malefactors, led with him to be put to death.

33. And when they were come to the place which is called Calvary, there they crucified him, and the malefactors; one on the right hand, and the other on the left.

34. Then said Jesus, Father, forgive them: for they know not what they do. And they parted his raiment, and cast lots.

35. And the people stood beholding. And the rulers also with them derided him, saying, He saved

others; let him save himself, if he be Christ, the chosen of God.

36. And the soldiers also mocked him, coming to him, and offering him vinegar,

37. And saying, If thou be the King of the Jews, save thyself.

38. And a superscription also was written over him, in letters of Greek, and Latin, and Hebrew, THIS IS THE KING OF THE JEWS.

39. And one of the malefactors, which were hanged, railed on him, saying, If thou be Christ, save thyself and us.

40. But the other answering, rebuked him, saying, Dost not thou fear God, seeing thou art in the same condemnation?

41. And we indeed justly; for we receive the due reward of our deeds: but this man hath done nothing amiss.

42. And he said unto Jesus, Lord, remember me when thou comest into thy kingdom.

43. And Jesus said unto him, Verily I say unto thee, To-day shalt thou be with me in paradise.

This is the story as it is found in the book written, according to tradition, by Luke—in Greek, *Lucas*. He was at no time supposed to be an apostle, but was, like Mark, a man of the next generation. Even Christian tradition, therefore, does not treat his statements as those of an eyewitness. There is a person of this name mentioned in two of the epistles of

Paul. If this person is the author of the Third Gospel, he probably was not a Jew originally, but a gentile convert—the first of that group we have so far encountered—and he was a physician. But to be a physician at that time implied no special social position or education. Some physicians had both but most of them did not, and a great many of them were slaves or freedmen.

The name tells us nothing, since it is an abbreviation of some Latin name beginning with *Luc*—Lucius, Lucianus, etc. Such names were very common among all classes of persons in the East, but they do not indicate Roman origin. Whatever we may be in doubt about, it is almost certain that the writer was Greek in speech.

But that the Lucas of the epistles is the author of our Third Gospel is after all merely a tradition. The writer nowhere names himself. It is a later tradition than the one about Mark. There is, however, some little force in the mere fact that the tradition existed. The credibility of the narrative could gain nothing from the mere fact of the ascription, since Luke was a friend of Paul who himself knew Jesus only by hearsay. And since it is merely a tradition we are not required to examine the personality of Luke as an absolute preliminary to the consideration of his evidence. For our purposes the book must be regarded as anonymous and its author indicated as "Luke," just as in the case of the other gospels.

Now, although the author does not name himself, he does do something which we do not find in the other gospels, but which we do find in a great many other ancient books. He prefixes a brief letter addressed to one Theophilus, apparently a recent convert, and in this letter he announces his purpose in writing the book. That purpose is to confirm the faith of the person addressed. We know therefore in this case what we can only have guessed before, that we have a complete and organized literary effort, meant to effect a specific object.

We must, however, not take for granted that because this book begins this way the whole book in our manuscripts was written by the author of the Preface. There is a certain initial probability that it was, if we allow for small changes and interpolations by copyists and commentators, but strange things happened to ancient books, particularly those which were afterward used for ritual purposes,

as this book was. For example, another book
of the New Testament already mentioned, the
Acts of the Apostles, is also addressed in a sentence to a Theophilus, and in that sentence the
author of Acts refers to a previous book similarly addressed. That has been very naturally
taken to prove that the author of Acts and of
"Luke" was the same. It is not at all impossible. But the book we call Acts contains large
portions which it is hard to believe belong to
the original form and in which the narrative is
told quite differently from the way it is told in
the other parts. So even if a definite and de-
terminable person wrote "Luke" for a definite
purpose as a single composition, we are not
thereby made sure that every part of our gospel was part of that single composition.

This Preface we must examine again. What
does "Luke" set out to do? Our version is un-
usually misleading, partly because the obsolete
and archaic English conveys a wrong impression to our minds, and partly because it is not
in any case a good translation. What "Luke"
really says may be paraphrased somewhat as
follows: "Many persons, my dear Theophilus,
have attempted to give a complete and orderly
account of the things we have seen accom-

plished in our time—an accomplishment which
we owe to those who saw its beginning and
ministered to its progress. Accordingly, I, too,
who have carefully followed the course of
events from their beginning, have decided to
write them out for you in sequence that you
may have an unfailing guide in the religion
into which you have been received." The
things "Luke" saw accomplished in his own
time was the existence of a large group of
Christian congregations spreading over all the
Mediterranean and especially in the East, and
this in what was after all an extremely short
time.

How does "Luke," with this purpose in
mind, tell the cardinal point in the story, the
account of the death of the Master, in whose
divine mission he and his pupil firmly believed?

He follows the main course of the story in
"Mark," but we cannot feel that he is merely
filling out gaps in that narrative or making deliberate modifications in it. He deals with it
with sufficient independence to make it likely
that, in this general outline, the story of Jesus'
trial and death had already become an accepted version; about which there might have
been conflicting details, but which in the main

was believed to have happened in the way described. The priests plotted his death, Judas
agreed to betray him for money. He was arrested on the night of the first Passover day,
tried before the high priest in the latter's
house, and taken to Pilate who made a fruit-
less effort to save him and finally ordered his
execution—a sentence immediately carried out
with the usual brutal circumstances. And the
words "King of the Jews" were written over
the cross.

But there is one important addition which
"Mark" does not mention at all. That is the
examination before Herod (23:7–11). This is,
of course, not the famous Herod, called the
Great, who died at about the time of the birth
of Christ, but his son, also called Herod and
surnamed Antipas—that is, "Little Antipater"
—after Herod's father, Antipater. Herod Antipas was tetrarch of Galilee, which means
that he had the power of king, with a somewhat less exalted title. In any case, however,
although a vassal of Rome, his territory was
not within the jurisdiction of a Roman magistrate. "Luke" tells us that Herod was in Jerusalem at the time, that Pilate as a courtesy
to him was willing to surrender Jesus to him,

that Herod examined Jesus but could get no
answer from him and finally declined to take
jurisdiction.

The incident is highly interesting. There is
nothing intrinsically improbable in it. Its details are neither inconsistent with one another
nor with anything else we know about the time
or the persons. It may well therefore have
literally happened just as "Luke" described it.
On the other hand, it may be a legend that developed in a period somewhat after Jesus'
death to explain why there was no conflict in
jurisdiction between the sovereign of Galilee to
which Jesus belonged and the Roman procurator. But in any case it can scarcely be an invention of "Luke's" who surely gives no indication of a disposition to fabricate whole incidents like this.

As a matter of fact, "Luke" gives us a special
reason for Pilate's action in regard to Herod.
Pilate and Herod had been enemies. As a result of this courtesy the two became friends.
Why Pilate should have desired a reconciliation
is not told us, but a previous incident mentioned by "Luke" himself may adequately account for the hostility; that is, Luke 13:1-4.
There Jesus refers to an incident which must

have been alive in the minds of his Galilean fellow-countrymen. On a previous Passover— how long ago we are not told—Pilate had caused a number of Galileans to be slaughtered so that their "blood was mingled with the sacrifice." This must accordingly have taken place at the very altar itself, and the horror of the incident was not mitigated by the fact that it was not the first act of brutal sacrilege of which Pilate had been guilty. Josephus mentions several, and though he does not mention this one—as no one else does—there is not the least reason to doubt that it was a real occurrence. But while a Judean writer like Josephus might neglect to note it, we may be sure that Galileans would not forget it nor would the tetrarch of Galilee, whose dignity had been affronted in this destruction of his lieges, however careless he might himself be of his subjects' lives or welfare. Why Pilate was contemptuously indifferent of Herod's rights on that occasion and why he was very anxious indeed not to repeat the offense we shall have occasion to examine later. But it cannot be denied that "Luke" is drawing on materials that have a ring of authenticity. His narrative hangs together.

There is another change in the general narrative. The time elapsed seems to "Luke" quite inadequate. According to "Mark" and "Matthew," Jesus was arrested on the evening of the first day of Passover, tried the same night, delivered to Pilate in the early morning of the next day, ordered to be immediately executed —an order carried out at once. And his death occurred before evening. Even without the Herod incident that was apparently too short a time in "Luke's" view. He either accepted a version in which the time was more extended or doubted the accuracy of the account sufficiently to make a conjecture that the time had really been longer. Jesus was not tried, according to "Luke," until the day following his arrest, and was delivered to Pilate later on that day. When he was sent to Herod and when he was sent back, when Pilate examined him and when he ordered his execution, does not appear with clearness. The only thing that seems inferable is that the feast of Passover was still on, since it was during the feast only that a prisoner was released (23:17). But the Passover lasted a week, so that there is abundant time for these things to have happened, even if each of them occupied a full day or more.

When we come to details, we must notice a number of differences. Again it is the chief priests and scribes who conspired against Jesus, and this time their hesitancy is unmistakably the fear of rousing popular resentment. In "Mark" and "Matthew" it was possible to suppose that it was the exceptional crowd on the first day of the Passover which alarmed them. Any arrest might cause a tumult. But in "Luke" the words seem to mean that they feared the popular following of Jesus, although it does not appear in the subsequent events that they had any reason for their fear.

Judas' treason is ascribed directly to literal possession by Satan. That this is intended, even in the slightest degree, to lighten his guilt is not likely but possible. Satan in the time of Jesus is, in popular belief, a devil, and not merely an accusing angel, as he is in the Book of Job. And possession by a devil is the ordinary explanation of madness, as is abundantly shown throughout the gospels. It is conceivable that "Luke" meant to state that Judas' betrayal was due to a fit of mental aberration. But Jesus' rebuke of Judas at the time of the arrest is against that supposition.

At any rate, we hear nothing of Judas again.

"Matthew's" story of the repentance is wholly absent. If "Luke" also wrote the Acts, the story of Judas' fate came down to him in a version different from that of Matthew. Certainly, as has been stated, the natural meaning of the words in Acts 1:25 is that Judas perished by an accident in the very field he had bought with his blood money. However, there may be significance in the fact that the author of Acts places the account in the mouth of a speaker, Peter, and does not state it as a part of his ordinary narrative. It is a little curious that in "Luke" when Judas appears with the priests to arrest Jesus (22:47) he is described as though he had not been mentioned before. That, it is true, is a difficulty which can easily be overcome. "Luke" may have wished by repeating that he was "one of the twelve" to emphasize the treason, as we may also suppose to have been the case in the story of "Mark" (14:43). But the expression "he that was called Judas" (Luke 22:47) is strange if it relates to a person already known in the story, and in no other place is such an expression used, when the ordinary name of a person is given and not some surname or descriptive epithet. It is possible that there is something wrong in the text.

Among those who appear to arrest Jesus there are not, as before, emissaries of the officials, but the "chief priests" themselves, and the elders. To them is added a new group, the "captains of the Temple." The title is an extraordinarily high one. It is the Greek *strategos*, properly "general," used ordinarily at that time not only for the local chief magistrates in provincial towns but even for the Roman praetor. We know from the oldest part of the Talmud, the Mishna—which was codified about A.D. 200, but most of which was written earlier—and from Josephus, that there was an officer in Jerusalem called by this high title. But there was only one, and he was a magistrate next in rank to the high priest. "Luke" speaks of many "captains," who can hardly have existed. "Mark" and "Matthew" know nothing of them but describe the arrest as though it had been carried out by subordinates.

And the place of the trial is differently described. It is again in the high priest's house. In "Mark" and "Matthew" the *aulē*, or court, is "outside" the Council Chamber (Matt. 26:69) or "below" it (Mark 14:66). In the court is a fire at which some slaves warm themselves. Here Peter, too, remains until he is recognized. But whereas in "Mark" and "Matthew" the sequence of events would lead one to suppose that the Council room opened directly on the *aulē*, that is not so in "Luke." The Peter incident took place on the night of the arrest. Peter gets as far as the *aulē* with the soldiers who have seized Jesus. The recognition and denial take place at once in the presence of Jesus himself and Peter withdraws. Jesus is then taken into the house and the next morning brought to the Council. Where he is kept and where the Council meets is not indicated, but the place had no relation to the *aulē* at all, nor was it conceivable that from the *aulē* the proceeding could be observed or its details followed. Accordingly, just as before, we have no evidence that any one of Jesus' adherents or friends was present at the trial. It is implied, to be sure, that there were slaves and attendants there, but these latter, as far as they are referred to, are represented as hostile.

What of Joseph of Arimathea? In "Luke's" account, as in "Mark" but not in "Matthew" (Luke 23:50–51), he is a counselor, *buleutēs*, a member of the Sanhedrin. He is even more, he is *buleutes hyparchon*, that is, actually serving in the capacity of member of the Sanhedrin. The implications of this fact are apparent to "Luke." How had Joseph voted in the Sanhedrin? The answer is (23:51): "The same [Joseph] had not consented to the counsel and deed of them." He must therefore have been absent, or voted for Jesus' acquittal. The latter supposition is rather opposed to the "all" of 22:70. For reasons already given we cannot think it probable that he was forced into voting against Jesus, and if we do not think of Joseph as present at the trial, we have in "Luke," just as in "Mark" and "Matthew," no clear statement of how the knowledge of the trial came to those who reported it.

A striking difference in the account of "Luke" is the absence of the high priest. He takes no part in the plotting, the trial, the delivery to Pilate, or the incitement of the mob. It is merely stated that the trial takes place in his palace. But he is not mentioned by name in this connection as in "Matthew," nor referred to individually as in "Mark." He does not rend his robe and cry "Blasphemy." If we did not know it from other sources, we should have no inkling that the high priest had any authority at all.

Caiaphas had been mentioned before (Luke 3:2), but that was in another connection. "Luke" there dates with an extraordinary precision the exact year in which John the Baptist first began to preach. It was in the fifteenth year of Tiberius, while Pontius Pilate was governor, Herod was tetrarch of Galilee, Philip was tetrarch of Iturea, Lysanias was tetrarch of Abilene, and while Annas and Caiaphas were high priests. The year of Tiberius gives us the date A.D. 27–28, which suits the other determinations well enough. But a double high priesthood is unintelligible. From what we know of Jewish organization we may set it down as impossible.

If we had no other information we might assume that the high priesthood changed that year and that Annas was high priest in the early part of it and was later displaced by Caiaphas. Yet, John's first preaching must have taken place either under the one or the other, and there is no example in which two successive magistrates are both named in dating a year. "Luke" apparently had the mistaken notion that the high priests, like the Roman consuls and other magistrates in cities which he knew, held office jointly. But in any case Caiaphas is mentioned as the high priest when John first appeared and nothing is said directly to indicate that he continued to be high priest when Jesus was arraigned, certainly nothing to show that it was he rather than Annas.

And upon closer scrutiny another thing appears. The examination before the chief priests and the Council is scarcely a trial even in form. The brutal jesting (22:63–64) takes place before Jesus is tried, not as in "Matthew" and "Mark," after the pronouncement of the verdict. No witnesses are examined. An indefinite number of the Council ask Jesus if he is the Messiah. Jesus' answer implies that he is, but he does not say so directly. To the further question of whether he claimed to be the Son of God, his answer was, "Ye say that I am."

Again, this is no admission in form, nor yet a denial. It is perhaps the same kind of contemptuous indifference to the judgment of the Sanhedrin as that which Socrates exhibited before the Athenian popular court. But clearly the members of the court would become indignant, and it can scarcely be gainsaid that there is an implied admission that Jesus had assumed or claimed the right to assume both designations. Technically, however, he had not confessed.

And we notice there is no formal condemnation. In the other two gospels the Sanhedrin answers the formal query of their president "Is this man guilty?" with the verdict "Guilty." In "Luke" there is none of that. There is what is apparently an informal questioning by a certain number of persons, followed by the determination to take him to Pilate.

A very important difference is the accusation. All the stress is laid on the terms "Messiah" and "Son of God." Not a word appears of the charge concerning the Temple. That charge, we may remember, occurs in both "Matthew" and "Mark" as the only specific accusation. Witnesses attest it, and Jesus is implicitly found guilty because it is remembered against him when he is suffering his punishment. It disappears completely in "Luke's" story.

Pilate does not appear as suddenly as he did in "Mark" and "Matthew." As has been stated, his governorship of Judea is mentioned when "Luke" is attempting to date the first preaching of John the Baptist. Therefore it is sufficient to mention him, on the assumption

which would be made as a matter of course
that he continued to be governor.

And it is before Pilate that in "Luke's" account a trial takes place—the only proceeding in the story before us which can be called
a trial. It is also carried on in a way much
more like that of ordinary trials. In "Mark"
and "Matthew," Pilate incontinently begins
his interrogation of the accused. He assumes
a charge—indeed, we should be tempted to
say he brings it himself. It is the charge of
having assumed the title of "King of the
Jews." The character of the proceedings is
completely inquisitorial. Not so "Luke." The
chief priests make an accusation of treason on
two counts, one that he sought to impede the
collection of tribute and the other that he had
assumed the royal title. "He said he was the
Annointed King." It is only the last accusation which interests Pilate and to which he asks
Jesus to plead. "Is this true? Are you the
King of the Jews?" We must understand "Do
you call yourself King of the Jews?" The
Greek is susceptible of being so understood.

And once more Jesus answers neither "Yes"
nor "No," but uses the words "Thou sayest
it." We cannot be sure how "Luke" wishes us

to take this statement, but it is evident that Pilate might understand it either as an admission or as a refusal to answer. This latter attitude of a provincial toward the Roman governor would be almost as serious as a confession of guilt.

But the priests make two charges. The first one was not mentioned before and is not mentioned again except so far as it is repeated in the statement (23:5) that Jesus had been continually inciting the people from his first ministry in Galilee to the present day. Why, if this charge was made, does it seem to have been ignored? It was not so serious as a charge that the style of "King" had been assumed, but it was dangerous enough. That it was false "Luke" implies, and I think we can conjecture that he meant us to understand that it was palpably false. Of course, his immediate audience—his Christian readers—would assume as much without evidence. But "Luke" apparently meant to stigmatize the bad faith of the accusers in bringing so notoriously false an accusation.

And that it was in fact notoriously false we may take for granted. The famous story of Jesus and the tribute money is told in "Mark"

(12:13–17) and "Matthew" (22:15–22) as well
as in "Luke" himself (20:20–26). Whether it
is literally true or not, it is at any rate a tradition which was meant to describe Jesus' complete indifference to purely political questions.
This political indifference must have been an
outstanding fact in his career. To "Luke" and
"Luke's" readers, intent both on glorifying
Jesus and on clearing him of any suggestion of
anti-Roman feeling, the accusation, trumped
up and absurd as it obviously was, is meant to
display the effrontery of the accusers. But on
the messiahship charge we are not much assisted by "Luke's" account. It is clear that a
Christian writing for Christians is in a difficult
position in regard to it. He does not wish to
deny categorically that Jesus assumed it, since
he firmly believes that Jesus was the Messiah.
Apparently he puts words into Jesus' mouth
which can be understood as follows: "I have
not so called myself but I am in fact the Messiah."

Was there any further testimony? "Luke"
does not say so. The accusations are vehemently renewed, he says, but that is all. And
yet on a specific accusation to which no cate-
gorical denial is offered Pilate announces that

he finds no guilt in the accused. If we accept this as a fact, we can account for it either as "Luke's" readers would by the overwhelming impression Jesus made on him, or by the governor's disinclination to incur popular odium by executing a popular leader, as he deemed Jesus to be.

A third possibility, that he would not willingly inflict a death sentence on an incompletely convicted man, may be disregarded. There is nothing in the figure of Pilate, as it has come down to us—as it must have come down to "Luke's" readers—to invest him with the character of an upright judge. What he exhibits is the vacillation of a weak judge. He does not wish to condemn. He does not wish to disregard the importunity of the priests. He therefore seeks to rid himself of the whole matter by declining jurisdiction in favor of Herod.

The examination before Herod can be called a trial even less than the hearing before the priests. Herod in "Luke's" description was an irresponsible despot, a gatherer of remarkable occurrences, eager to see strange things, a miracle—a *semeion*—which would be a form of entertainment like any other piece of magic.

It was not the first time that Herod had

heard of Jesus. It is stated in all three gospels that news of Jesus' preaching had come to the tetrarch of Galilee. Indeed, it would be almost inconceivable to suppose that it had not, even if Jesus was only one of many such preachers and prophets. In both "Mark" (6:15) and "Luke" (9:8) the rumor is given that he is the reincarnate Elijah, or some other prophet. And "Luke" makes a distinct connection between this statement and this later incident by declaring that the tetrarch was eager to see the wonder-working teacher.

What happened when he saw him? Given the character of Herod, "Luke's" account is perfectly consistent. There is nothing like an examination. Herod asks questions. What questions? The context seems to indicate that they related rather to his reputed miracles than to anything of the specific charges brought. Evidently he desired Jesus to do a miracle in his presence.

We may suppose that the violent accusations which were repeated before Herod were to the same effect as before Pilate. Jesus was depicted as a rebel against the Roman authority which Herod represented as well as Pilate.

And when Jesus would neither answer his

questions nor perform miracles for his amuse-
ment, we can easily suppose that Herod
avenged himself as our text says he did, that
he abused his prisoner and jeered at him and
sent him back with mock ceremony, an act
which he meant to be a courtesy to Pilate and
which Pilate evidently accepted as a courtesy,
disinclined as he may have been to condemn
Jesus.

The Herod incident again presents the problem of source. Where did the narrator of this
story discover what had gone on in Herod's
house? We may conjecture as before that it
might have been a repentant accuser, or else
one of Herod's entourage, one of the military
attendants mentioned in 23:11. Both are possibilities, but they are gratuitous as far as
"Luke" is concerned, since he gives no hint
about it.

When the examination was resumed before
Pilate, the latter definitely pronounced Jesus
not guilty of the specific charge of treason.
Pilate says that he had questioned Jesus in
their presence and found no basis for the
charge. But in the first part of the examination Pilate had asked only one question and to
that Jesus had not really replied at all. Shall

we assume that there is a gap in our text or that "Luke" had forgotten the fact just stated? It is scarcely necessary. To men to whom any accusation against Jesus was a heinous sin, it would need explanation that his judge declared him guiltless.

But on what "Luke" tells us the acquittal is hard to understand. If Pilate did not take the accusation seriously because he believed the motive to be malice of the priests, it would be more intelligible, but while "Mark" and "Matthew" say that Pilate felt in this way about the accusation, "Luke" says nothing of the kind. He merely asserts that Pilate was convinced of the innocence of the accused after an examination and yielded to a pressure which just then it would not have been politic for a Roman governor to withstand. Our only difficulty is that the assertion omits the specific question asked of Jesus and not denied. If a claim to be Messiah was treason, we cannot tell how Pilate reached the conviction of Jesus' innocence.

The position of the mob is different. In "Mark's" account—still more in "Matthew's" —the mob is inside the praetorium, and has come there of its own accord, to demand the

customary pardon of a malefactor. It would
not need this excuse for an assemblage. Any
trial could draw a crowd, if it was in a place
into which a crowd could get. But in this case
Pilate calls together the chief priests, the
rulers, and the people. "Rulers" is, in Greek,
archontes, which is the ordinary term for magistrates. Perhaps "Luke" thought the "elders,"
the members of the Sanhedrin, were also magistrates. But if there had been a summoning of
the people it must have been done by something like a proclamation.

When Pilate continued his efforts to save
Jesus, he conferred with all these three groups
at once, and it is "they" who demand Bar-
Abbas and cry out for the crucifixion of
Jesus.

Pilate, however, still went on with his attempt. He asserted that Herod too had acquitted Jesus. He may have inferred this from
the fact that Jesus was sent back to him, but
if we recall "Luke's" story of how Herod had
sent him back, the inference is scarcely justified. The mock semiroyal ceremonial would
indicate that the title of "king" had really been
assumed. It may further be noted that if
Herod had accepted jurisdiction and acquitted

Jesus of any crime Jesus would have been set free by that determination alone.

But Pilate after all did not say that Jesus was guiltless. Whether he wished to compromise or not, he asserted merely that Jesus had committed no crime deserving of death. In his statement concerning Herod he repeats this conclusion, disguised though it is under an obvious mistranslation in both the Authorized and Revised Version of the New Testament. "Nothing worthy of death has been done unto him," makes little sense in this context. We should rather read (23:15): "No, nor yet Herod [has found fault with this man], for I sent you to him and lo, nothing deserving death has been done by him [Jesus]." Pilate states Herod's conclusion as a fact, as is done so commonly.

The implication is that Pilate accepts the accusers' statement that an offense has been committed, but he will not deem it a capital one. He proposes therefore a milder punishment of scourging, a scourging which will be far short of the kind of scourging which precedes crucifixion. The word used in the Greek text was a euphemism for this penalty. Compared with Pilate's first statement (23:6), "I find no fault with this man," it has all the air of a compromise. If it was so, it was rejected by the priests and people.

There is an implication which may be an inadvertence in the narrative, but may possibly be intentional. In "Matthew" and "Mark" the proposal that Jesus and not Bar-Abbas be released is clearly a substitution of one condemned man for another. That substitution is not so clearly put in "Luke." Pilate offers to have Jesus scourged and released. If we assume that the crowd accepted Jesus as the person to be pardoned, there would certainly have been no justification for scourging. We may take it that Pilate, according to "Luke," offered to release Bar-Abbas unconditionally, although his guilt was beyond question and also to inflict the milder punishment on Jesus, whose guilt he only reluctantly admitted if at all. In other words, both the priests and people were bitterly hostile to Jesus and we cannot infer, as we could before, from the popular clamor that they merely preferred the more popular Bar-Abbas. This is borne out by the fact that there is no mention here of any trick on the part of the priests to insure Jesus' death by inciting the people to cry for Bar-Abbas, as is the case in "Mark" and "Matthew." The people do so of their own accord, and when "Luke" contrasts Jesus and Bar-Abbas, it is to compare the fate of an innocent man and that of a seditious one to the discredit of those who created this contrast.

And, finally, there is a marked difference in the manner of the execution. "Mark" and "Matthew" represent it as carried out by the Roman soldiery with brutality and ribaldry. "Luke" evidently thinks that it was the Jewish authorities that actually carried out the Crucifixion. Even if the phrase "he delivered Jesus to their will" may bear the meaning "in accordance with their will," the rest of the description seems to show the Jews as the executioners. To be sure, the derisive inscription, which in "Mark" is not necessarily meant to be derisive—"This is the King of the Jews" (23:38)—is not what one might expect the priests to have put there, but "Luke's" belief about it is fairly clear.

If one can draw any general inferences, they may be the following: "Luke" has a completely different notion of the organization of the Judean community from the notion of "Mark" and "Matthew." The high priest is apparently a titular office; the elders are magistrates; there is a military organization of the Temple guard, under a group of men called "captains." The priests and magistrates, however, act in matters like this rather as accusers than as judges —accusers who press insistently for judgment on the testimony they have suborned. The whole responsibility of Jesus' death is thus put on the heads of the Jews since Pilate fails to save Jesus after exhausting every reasonable effort to do so.

That the inconsistencies between "Luke" and our non-biblical sources are somewhat more troublesome than in the case of the first two gospels may be due to the fact that this book is more openly and consciously a book of edification, addressed to a recent convert, and if the tradition is accurate, written by a gentile convert. It is not an attempt to clear the memory of Jesus from the charges against him, by a defense written like Xenophon's *Memorabilia of Socrates* for the general public. "Luke's" public has no doubt of the innocence, formal and substantial, of their Master.

The tendency to exculpate the Romans becomes one of the principal marks of the story. "Luke's" public and "Luke" himself could not accept the statement that Jesus' assumption of the titles "Messiah," "King," and "Son of God" was a crime. But "Luke" considered perversion of the people and sedition a crime, and, like other Christian writers, is very eager to show that neither Jesus nor his followers could be held guilty of it. For that reason he cites as the sole evidence against Jesus a preposterously false statement about him.

Whether when "Luke" differs from "Mark" or "Matthew" he is entitled to greater credibility must be determined by other considerations. The balance of probability is against him in some matters if for no other reason than the avowed religious and didactic purpose of the book.

CHAPTER IV

JOHN

11:47. Then gathered the chief priests and the Pharisees a council, and said, What do we? for this man doeth many miracles.

48. If we let him thus alone, all men will believe on him: and the Romans shall come, and take away both our place and nation.

49. And one of them, named Caiaphas, being the high priest that same year, said unto them, Ye know nothing at all,

50. Nor consider that it is expedient for us, that one man should die for the people, and that the whole nation perish not.

51. And this spake he not of himself: but being high priest that year, he prophesied that Jesus should die for that nation;

52. And not for that nation only, but that also he should gather together in one the children of God that were scattered abroad.

53. Then from that day forth they took counsel together for to put him to death.

54. Jesus therefore walked no more openly among the Jews; but went thence unto a country near to the wilderness, into a city called Ephraim, and there continued with his disciples.

55. And the Jews' passover was nigh at hand; and

many went out of the country up to Jerusalem before the passover, to purify themselves.

56. Then sought they for Jesus, and spake among themselves, as they stood in the temple, What think ye, that he will not come to the feast?

57. Now both the chief priests and the Pharisees had given a commandment, that, if any man knew where he were, he should shew it, that they might take him.

13: 1. Now before the feast of the passover, when Jesus knew that his hour was come that he should depart out of this world unto the Father, having loved his own which were in the world, he loved them unto the end.

2. And supper being ended, the devil having now put him into the heart of Judas Iscariot, Simon's son, to betray him.

3. Jesus knowing that the Father had given all things into his hands, and that he was come from God, and went to God:

21. When Jesus had thus said, he was troubled in spirit, and testified, and said, Verily, verily, I say unto you, that one of you shall betray me.

22. Then the disciples looked one on another, doubting of whom he spake.

23. Now there was leaning on Jesus' bosom, one of his disciples, whom Jesus loved.

24. Simon Peter therefore beckoned to him, that he should ask who it should be of whom he spake.

25. He then, lying on Jesus' breast, said unto him, Lord, who is it? Jesus answered, He it is whom I shall give a sop, when I have dipped it. And when he had dipped the sop, he gave it to Judas Iscariot, the son of Simon.

26. And after the sop Satan entered into him. Then said Jesus unto him, That thou doest, do quickly.

27. Now no man at the table knew for what intent he spake this unto him.

28. For some of them thought, because Judas had the bag, that Jesus had said unto him,

29. Buy those things that we have need of against the feast; or, that he should give something to the poor.

30. He then, having received the sop, went immediately out: and it was night.

18: 1. When Jesus had spoken these words, he went forth with his disciples over the brook Cedron, where was a garden, into which he entered, and his disciples.

2. And Judas also, which betrayed him, knew the place: for Jesus oft-times resorted thither with his disciples.

3. Judas then, having received a band of men and officers from the chief priests and Pharisees, cometh thither with lanterns, and torches, and weapons.

4. Jesus therefore, knowing all things that should come upon him, went forth, and said unto them, Whom seek ye?

5. They answered him, Jesus of Nazareth. Jesus saith unto them, I am he. And Judas also, which betrayed him, stood with them.

6. As soon then as he had said unto them, I am he, they went backward, and fell to the ground.

7. Then asked he them again, Whom seek ye? And they said, Jesus of Nazareth.

8. Jesus answered, I have told you that I am he. If therefore ye seek me, let these go their way:

9. That the saying might be fulfilled which he spake, Of them which thou gavest me, have I lost none.

10. Then Simon Peter, having a sword, drew it, and smote the high priest's servant, and cut off his right ear. The servant's name was Malchus.

11. Then said Jesus unto Peter, Put up thy sword into the sheath: the cup which my Father hath given me, shall I not drink it?

12. Then the band, and the captain, and officers of the Jews took Jesus, and bound him,

13. And led him away to Annas first, for he was father-in-law to Caiaphas, which was the high priest that same year.

14. Now Caiaphas was he which gave counsel to the Jews, that it was expedient that one man should die for the people.

15. And Simon Peter followed Jesus, and so did another disciple. That disciple was known unto the high priest, and went in with Jesus, into the palace of the high priest.

16. But Peter stood at the door without. Then went out that other disciple which was known

unto the high priest, and spake unto her that kept the door, and brought in Peter.

17. Then saith the damsel that kept the door unto Peter, Art thou not also one of this man's disciples? He saith, I am not.

18. And the servants and officers stood there, who had made a fire of coals, for it was cold; and they warmed themselves: and Peter stood with them, and warmed himself.

19. The high priest then asked Jesus of his disciples, and of his doctrine.

20. Jesus answered him, I spake openly to the world; I ever taught in the synagogue, and in the temple, whither the Jews resort always; and in secret have I said nothing.

21. Why askest thou me? ask them which heard me, what I have said unto them: behold, they know what I said.

22. And when he had thus spoken, one of the officers which stood by, struck Jesus with the palm of his hand, saying, Answerest thou the high priest so?

23. Jesus answered him, If I have spoken evil, bear witness of the evil: but if well, why smitest thou me?

24. Now Annas had sent him bound unto Caiaphas the high priest.

25. And Simon Peter stood and warmed himself. They said therefore unto him, Art not thou also one of his disciples? He denied it, and said, I am not.

26. One of the servants of the high priest, being his kinsman whose ear Peter cut off, saith, Did not I see thee in the garden with him?

27. Peter then denied again: and immediately the cock crew.

28. Then led they Jesus from Caiaphas unto the hall of judgment: and it was early; and they themselves went not into the judgment hall, lest they should be defiled; but that they might eat the passover.

29. Pilate then went out unto them, and said, What accusation bring ye against this man?

30. They answered and said unto him, If he were not a malefactor, we would not have delivered him unto thee.

31. Then said Pilate unto them, Take ye him, and judge him according to your law. The Jews therefore said unto him, It is not lawful for us to put any man to death:

32. That the saying of Jesus might be fulfilled, which he spake, signifying what death he should die.

33. Then Pilate entered into the judgment hall again, and called Jesus, and said unto him, Art thou the King of the Jews?

34. Jesus answered him, Sayest thou this thing of thyself, or did others tell it thee of me?

35. Pilate answered, Am I a Jew? Thine own nation, and the chief priests, have delivered thee unto me. What hast thou done?

36. Jesus answered, My kingdom is not of this world: if my kindgom were of this world, then

would my servants fight, that I should not be
delivered to the Jews: but now is my kingdom
not from hence.

37. Pilate therefore said unto him, Art thou a king
then? Jesus answered, Thou sayest that I am a
king. To this end was I born, and for this cause
came I into the world, that I should bear witness unto the truth. Every one that is of the
truth, heareth my voice.

38. Pilate saith unto him, What is truth? And when
he had said this, he went out again unto the
Jews, and saith unto them, I find in him no
fault at all.

39. But ye have a custom that I should release unto
you one at the passover: will ye therefore, that
I release unto you the King of the Jews?

40. Then cried they all again, saying, Not this man,
but Barabbas. Now Barabbas was a robber.

19: 1. Then Pilate therefore took Jesus, and scourged
him.

2. And the soldiers platted a crown of thorns, and
put it on his head, and they put on him a purple
robe.

3. And said, Hail, King of the Jews! and they smote
him with their hands.

4. Pilate therefore went forth again, and saith unto
them, Behold, I bring him forth to you, that
ye may know that I find no fault in him.

5. Then came Jesus forth, wearing the crown of
thorns, and the purple robe. And Pilate saith
unto them, Behold the man!

6. When the chief priests therefore and officers saw him, they cried out, saying, Crucify him, crucify him. Pilate saith unto them, Take ye him, and crucify him: for I find no fault in him.

7. The Jews answered him, We have a law, and by our law he ought to die, because he made himself the Son of God.

8. When Pilate therefore heard that saying, he was the more afraid;

9. And went again into the judgment-hall, and saith unto Jesus, Whence art thou? But Jesus gave him no answer.

10. Then saith Pilate unto him, Speakest thou not unto me? knowest thou not, that I have power to crucify thee, and have power to release thee?

11. Jesus answered, Thou couldest have no power at all against me, except it were given thee from above: therefore he that delivered me unto thee hath the greater sin.

12. And from thenceforth Pilate sought to release him: but the Jews cried out, saying, If thou let this man go, thou art not Cesar's friend. Whosoever maketh himself a king, speaketh against Cesar.

13. When Pilate therefore heard that saying, he brought Jesus forth, and sat down in the judgment-seat, in a place that is called the Pavement, but in the Hebrew, Gabbatha.

14. And it was the preparation of the passover, and he saith unto the Jews, Behold your King!

15. But they cried out, Away with him, away with him, crucify him. Pilate saith unto them, Shall

I crucify your King? The chief priests answered, We have no king but Cesar.

16. Then delivered he him therefore unto them to be crucified. And they took Jesus and led him away.

17. And he bearing his cross went forth into a place called the place of a skull, which is called in the Hebrew, Golgotha:

18. Where they crucified him, and two others with him, on either side one, and Jesus in the midst.

19. And Pilate wrote a title, and put it on the cross. And the writing was, JESUS OF NAZARETH, THE KING OF THE JEWS.

20. This title then read many of the Jews: for the place where Jesus was crucified was nigh to the city: and it was written in Hebrew, and Greek, and Latin.

21. Then said the chief priests of the Jews to Pilate, Write not, The King of the Jews; but that he said, I am King of the Jews.

22. Pilate answered, What I have written, I have written.

23. Then the soldiers, when they had crucified Jesus, took his garments, and made four parts, to every soldier a part; and also his coat: now the coat was without seam, woven from the top throughout.

24. They said therefore among themselves, Let us not rend it, but cast lots for it whose it shall be: that the scripture might be fulfilled, which saith, They parted my raiment among them, and for

my vesture they did cast lots. These things
therefore the soldiers did.

25. Now there stood by the cross of Jesus, his
mother, and his mother's sister, Mary the wife
of Cleophas, and Mary Magdalene.

26. When Jesus therefore saw his mother, and the
disciple standing by whom he loved, he saith
unto his mother, Woman, behold thy son!

27. Then saith he to the disciple, Behold thy mother!
And from that hour that disciple took her unto
his own home.

28. After this, Jesus knowing that all things were
now accomplished, that the scripture might be
fulfilled, saith, I thirst.

29. Now there was set a vessel full of vinegar: and
they filled a sponge with vinegar, and put it
upon hyssop, and put it to his mouth.

30. When Jesus therefore had received the vinegar,
he said, It is finished: and he bowed his head,
and gave up the ghost.

31. The Jews therefore, because it was the preparation, that the bodies should not remain upon the
cross on the sabbath-day, (for that sabbath-day
was an high day) besought Pilate that their legs
might be broken, and that they might be taken
away.

32. Then came the soldiers, and brake the legs of
the first, and of the other which was crucified
with him.

33. And when they came to Jesus, and saw that he
was dead already, they brake not his legs.

34. But one of the soldiers with a spear pierced his side, and forthwith came thereout blood and water.

35. And he that saw it, bare record, and his record is true: and he knoweth that he saith true, that ye might believe.

36. For these things were done, that the scripture should be fulfilled, A bone of him shall not be broken.

37. And again another scripture saith, They shall look on him whom they pierced.

38. And after this, Joseph of Arimathea (being a disciple of Jesus, but secretly for fear of the Jews) besought Pilate that he might take away the body of Jesus: and Pilate gave him leave. He came therefore and took the body of Jesus.

In discussing "John's" account the question of authorship is again of primary importance. The historical John was not merely an apostle but in very early church traditions one of the foremost of the apostles, vying with Peter for primacy. Another book, which has also been taken into our Bible, the Apocalypse or Book of Revelation, was ascribed to him. An early account in a wholly different part of the Bible, the Acts, speaks of his prominence in the first Christian church, that of Jerusalem, and of his outstanding importance in the first great field of Christian missions, which was Asia Minor.

Tradition could say something of even greater moment about him. It was said that he was the best beloved of Jesus' disciples and in a sense his heir, since Jesus intrusted the guardianship of his mother to him. This may be a later development and may be based on a passage in "John" itself (19:25-27). But it is possible also that it was of independent origin, and the existence of such a tradition makes it particularly important to reach some conclusion on the question of authorship at once.

As in the case of "Matthew," we note that nowhere is there any direct statement of who the author is. Even if 19:25-27 does refer to John, it merely means that in the author's mind John is the first of the apostles and the real heir of Jesus. If John wrote the Fourth Gospel he was an eyewitness of many of the things he reports. Yet he never mentions that fact. This is the more curious because, as the text cited shows, he frequently speaks of the testimony of other eyewitnesses. It is so curious, indeed, that if we knew nothing of the tradition of Johannine authorship, we should, I think, have inferred from a cursory reading that whoever wrote the Gospel could not have been a direct associate of Jesus and therefore could not have seen John.

I may say at once that biblical critics are practically unanimous in denying John's authorship, many of them even going so far as to class the Gospel with the so-called "Gospel of Peter" and other demonstrably late compilations, as one of the apocryphal gospels. The reasons are many, and to trained historians conclusive, and several of them may be mentioned.

There is, first of all, the strong intrinsic improbability that a book like the Fourth Gospel, full of a special sort of theosophical theory, could have been written by a Galilean fisherman. This theosophy is contained in the Logos doctrine which is not found in "John's" story of the Passion, but is set forth in other passages, particularly in the famous exordium (1:1), "In the beginning was the Word." We know a great deal of this "Logos doctrine, and of the people who expounded it. It has affinities with Hindu Vedantism and with many forms of mysticism of Europe and Asia, and it was particularly associated with the mystical development of Platonism of which we see so much in the work of the Alexandrian Jew,

Philo. It is a doctrine of bookish men, of semi-monkish illuminati. There is not a word about it in any other gospel or in any other part of the New Testament. That such a doctrine should have its exclusive proponent among our biblical writers a man who in all probability must have been scarcely literate is well-nigh impossible.

Second, there is the fact that "John's" statements in regard to the life of his time and the physical background are more confused than that of any other gospel and more pronouncedly at variance with our non-biblical information. If "John" of all the disciples wrote this book, we should expect just the opposite.

Finally, Christian literature almost up to the end of the second century is apparently silent about any gospel or any memoirs of Jesus written by John, although there are many statements about John and there is a fairly early tradition about the other gospels.

These are weighty objections when we remember that even if they did not exist we should still be wholly without any evidence whatever that John actually did write the passages which introduce this chapter or the book in which they are contained. In the case of

"Matthew," absence of such evidence made it necessary to proceed on the hypothesis that Matthew was not the author of the gospel of that name. In the case of "John," the evidence is not merely negative but leans heavily to the other side.

Indeed, we can see that both the first and fourth gospels present greater difficulties in respect of the authenticity of their traditional authorship than the second and third. The fact that these are ascribed to Mark and Luke is in itself a point in favor of authenticity, although it cannot be called conclusive. There is no apparent reason why just these names should have been selected, unless in many Christian communities there were early versions of Jesus' life current, which bore the names of these men. But if there were also anonymous versions current, or if a later writer prepared an account of Jesus' life and ministry, there was a great temptation to use the name of one known to have been a personal associate of Jesus. We need not assume fraudulent intent.

The ascription may have been a guess at first, repeated until it became current. In the same way among the Greeks, dialogues were ascribed to Plato and orations to Demosthenes

which were not written by them, and a great
deal of Alexandrian scholarship was occupied
in discriminating between genuine works of
the great masters and those which had acci-
dentally crept into collections of these genuine
works.

And even if a later writer deliberately put
John's name to his own composition, that involves none of the moral turpitude which
would attach to such an act today. It was no
infrequent literary device in ancient days to
do so. Books of that sort—called by the long
word "pseudepigraphical"—were recognized
forms of giving currency to special doctrines,
particularly in religious controversies. Whatever may be the result now, when they were
published they were not really intended to deceive.

Let us now examine just how the writer,
whom we must call "John" for brevity, imagined
the trial and death of Jesus.

There is a certain amount of similarity of
outline. It may be thus summarized: the plot
by the priests, the arrest of Jesus on the Passover through the treachery of Judas, the examination before the high priest, the examination before Pilate who makes futile efforts to

save him, the demand of priests and people for his crucifixion and for the release of Bar-Abbas and the actual execution with the inscription of "King of the Jews" on the cross.

But if this is the outline the details are in many cases strikingly different. First of all the plotters are different. It is not the chief priests and the elders—that is to say, the religious and civil authorities of the people—but the chief priests and the Pharisees who call a meeting to plan the death of Jesus and who have him arrested. Later on, it is a group vaguely specified as "they" and including by enumeration merely the high priest—perhaps the chief priests—and those whom our version calls "officers," but who in the Greek text are called *hypēretai*, "servants." Whether it is implied that the Pharisees are there too we cannot be sure, but in any case the part they play in the earlier stages gives us pause.

The Pharisees appear in the other gospels as one of several Jewish sects. They are nowhere identified with the scribes or elders or put in any particular association with the chief priests. That is just the status of the Pharisees in the other sources of our knowledge about them, the earlier part of the Talmud (Mishna) and in Josephus who was himself a Pharisee and who lived in the latter part of the first century A.D.

In the first three gospels the Pharisees are represented as almost uniformly hostile to Jesus and bitterly denounced by him. It is not quite uniform, because in at least one instance one of the chief Pharisees is the host of Jesus and is therefore in all likelihood in friendly sympathy with him. But it is none the less true that the most severe of the denunciations put in the mouth of Jesus are in these gospels directed against the Pharisees. We must take it accordingly that if "Matthew," "Mark," or "Luke" had known of any story which described Jesus' death to their plotting, that story would have been told. The fact that it is not even hinted is in this instance strong evidence that the first three gospels did not know it. It looks for all the world like the conception of a later writer who composed his account when the Pharisees became the dominant sect among the Jews and so represented the Jews as a nation, an event which took place in the second century, long after the death of Jesus, when the final rebellion of the Palestinian Jews caused the complete destruction of the last vestiges of their autonomy.

The other actors in "John" are strangely unlike those of the same name in the other gospels. Judas is more specifically described. His patronymic is given as "the son of Simon" (12:4). He is stated to have been a hypocrite and an embezzler. He leads the band which comes to arrest Jesus, but he does not greet him and he immediately disappears from the narrative. And, curiously enough, not a word is said at any time of the thirty pieces of silver or of any compensation to Judas, nor is there any reference to his repentance and suicide.

We can scarcely believe that "John" knew very much about the Judas incident in spite of the insertion of the patronymic—which may well have been invented *ad hoc* as appears to be the case with the name of the high priest's servant, Malchus, who had his ear severed by Peter.

Then there is Caiaphas. He is first mentioned (11:49) as one of "them," that is, of the "chief priests," to which is added the phrase "being the high priest that same year." The translation is misleading; the Greek very plainly says "being the High Priest for that year," since it is evidently "John's" notion that the high priesthood was an annual office like nearly all the municipal magistracies of the

Roman Empire, some of which were priesthoods also. The same phrase is repeated in the same obvious sense in 18:13. But in any case Caiaphas is made to speak with nothing less than divine inspiration—"not of himself" (11:51). A different version of Caiaphas' inspiration seems to underlie the repetition of that statement (18:14); although what is ascribed to Caiaphas is not hostile to Jesus in form, but whether sincere or feigned it is merely a pronouncement that it is better for one man to perish than for the people to do so—a pronouncement which one can almost say "John" approves.

Caiaphas does not seem himself to have brought Jesus to Pilate. In fact, he is not mentioned after the examination of Jesus. All the rest of the evil done to Jesus is done by "them," whom we may guess to be the chief priests and the Pharisees, but who, as far as anything is told us to the contrary, may just as well be the last group mentioned as a group, the military and other attendants of the high priest, the "band and captain and officers of the Jews." The terms used are *speira*, which generally means a Roman cohort, and *chiliarchos*, which generally means the Roman military tribune, a rather high officer. In any case "John" supposes the Jews to have a military organization of their own, quite apart from that of the Romans, since the words he uses have an almost exclusively military sense. The only way in which "they" are specified at all is by the word "Jews" (19:12), and later it appears that the chief priests are among them (19:15).

Caiaphas has not very much direct concern with the trial, and another and a quite-new figure has apparently even less. The Jewish troops first bring Jesus bound to "Annas, for he was father in law to Caiaphas" (18:13). That seems no good reason, especially as in the passages immediately following it is Caiaphas and not Annas who examines Jesus, and it is only by an apparent afterthought that we are suddenly informed (18:24) that Annas had sent him to Caiaphas.

But although we do not clearly see the functions of Caiaphas or of Annas, one thing stands out at once: There is no Sanhedrin at all. That is to say, there is no trial in any sense, and no condemnation. Caiaphas examines Jesus personally and asks him about his disciples and his doctrines. Jesus declines to answer and is beaten by a servant for his alleged insolence. But Caiaphas has really brought no accusation of any kind, not the accusation about tearing down and rebuilding the Temple or that about claiming to be Messiah and Son of God.

This omission must be deliberate, for Pilate calls "their" attention to the fact that no accusation has been made against him. Their reply is plainly in bad faith, and they counter Pilate's suggestion that they deal with Jesus themselves, by declining jurisdiction.

Pilate, however, does put before Jesus the charge as he infers it, that he claims to be king. Jesus first pleads what is in effect a denial, but a few verses later repeats the evasive answer which the other gospels put in his mouth. And here, as in the others, we can note an evident intention of clearing Pilate from any large share in his death. He leaves the "judgment hall" three times to confer with the accusers in order to attempt to free Jesus. Once he offers to leave the matter wholly in their hands; a second time he offers to pardon Jesus in honor of the feast; and a third time he is almost awed into releasing him at once, and yields only to a threat of being denounced as a traitor. But if Pilate is not made to bear the burden of putting Jesus to death, there is no attempt to make something of a half-Christian out of him. He says that he "finds no fault" in Jesus, but he has him scourged even while saying so, and there is nothing to indicate that he intends the scourging to be a milder punishment in order to satisfy Jesus' bitter enemies by a compromise. In fact, Pilate is irresolute and almost irrational since his last question "Whence art thou?" comes at a most unexpected stage of the proceedings; and he is about to release Jesus just as the latter has specifically declared that the Jews and not the Roman governor will be primarily guilty of his death. The term used is the singular (19:12) and may possibly mean the high priest.

The Sanhedrin did not appear to try him, and nothing shows us that in the Bar-Abbas incident it is the mob which rejects Jesus. Apparently the people asked are the same "they" who brought Jesus bound from Caiaphas' house and who continue their persecution of him. Bar-Abbas too is dismissed with a brief "Now, Bar-Abbas was a robber," although the other gospels had stated that he was an insurgent chief. This deprives the incident of its normal rationale. It was natural that the Jerusalem mob should prefer the leader of an insurrection to Jesus, or indeed to most other condemned men. The priests and Pharisees may have wished to reject Jesus but there is no suggestion to explain why they selected an ordinary robber to be the recipient of a pardon.

The difficulty about how "John" knows what took place before the high priest disappears in this version. Not only Peter but another disciple was actually in the room with Jesus and Caiaphas. It is stated that this other disciple was known to the high priest. This detail is seemingly added to explain how he managed to enter so easily and even to bring Peter in. We must assume he was not known to be a disciple, for otherwise the high priest's question about Jesus' disciples is scarcely reasonable. That is probably what "John" means us to infer, but he does not say so, although in the case of Joseph of Arimathea he states that Joseph was in secret a disciple. It is of course equally possible that the detail was added merely to give a background to the Peter incident and perhaps to lower Peter somewhat in favor of the other and unnamed disciple. We may note, by the way, that noth-

ing is said of Joseph's membership in the Sanhedrin. And yet the story of the unnamed
disciple cannot after all have been added in
order to meet the difficulty which we noted
before, about the writer's source of information concerning the trial, because there is
nothing to report. There is no meeting, no
trial, no deposition of witnesses, no rending of
robes, and no condemnation. A single question
is asked of Jesus who gives a longer reply than
he is elsewhere credited with uttering and is
struck by an attendant for insolence.

This part of the narrative, therefore, is notably different from the other narrative. There
is also a difference in time. All the other gospels placed the arrest on the night of the first
day of the Passover and the execution therefore on the second or even a later day of the
festival. It is important because it is the meal
of the first day which Jesus takes with his followers and which becomes the "Last Supper."
But "John" puts all the events—the meal, the
examination before Pilate, the execution—on
the "preparation for the Passover," that is to
say the day before, or perhaps the days before.
It has been conjectured that "John" changes
the date because he somewhere learned that

the Sanhedrin never sat on a feast day and therefore that Jesus could not have been condemned. It has even been taken to be one of the few cases in which "John's" version is historically more exact than that of the others. But this suggestion loses any value when we recall that "John" says nothing of a Sanhedrin, a trial before it, or even shows any knowledge that such a body existed as a formal and organized institution.

Nor can we really say that the putting of the Sanhedrin trial on the feast day—the very first day—is an error of the first three gospels. We are told merely in our Jewish sources about the Sanhedrin that the Sanhedrin held no regular or formal meeting on such a day. But "Mark" and "Matthew" do not describe the meeting as an ordinary one, but as a hasty convocation made by the high priest at night. If it was illegal, that would give greater point to "Mark's" contention that all the proceedings against Jesus were formally as well as substantially irregular. The high priest and his Council are represented throughout as unscrupulous men determined to hurry an innocent victim to his death.

It is more probable that "John" selected the

"preparation" rather than the Passover itself as the time of the attack on Jesus, because of a widespread notion in the gentile world that all Jewish feasts were Sabbaths of a kind and that the Jews abstained on them from nearly everything. John's misinformation on these details is nowhere better evidenced than in the statement (18:28): "And they themselves went not into the judgment hall, lest they should be defiled but that they might eat the passover." We are acquainted to an unusual extent with the rules of festival pollution and ritual purity which prevailed among the Jews at that time. There was none which forbade contact with Gentiles on this occasion. In fact, Gentiles were freely admitted to sacrifice at the Temple at Passover and many of them did so. Nor was entry into a gentile house or a gentile place or resort forbidden either before the feast or during it.

More pronouncedly than in "Luke," "John" makes the actual execution the deed of the Jewish authorities, forgetting that, as he himself knew, they had no legal power to inflict capital punishment. Indeed, it must have been common knowledge that nowhere in the Roman Empire where a Roman magistrate had jurisdiction, could capital punishment be inflicted except by him. The soldiers mentioned in 19:23–24 seem to be Roman soldiers, but their presence is hard to make out, if the execution is carried out by the Jews. But, after all, the soldiers are apparently dragged in to apply the prophecy about casting lots, which must have already become a permanent part of the story of the Passion. Again it is Pilate who determines the inscription on the cross, over the protest of the chief priests, so that he seems after all to retain control of the proceedings.

Thus, if we take the narrative as a whole, reading it consecutively without reference to the other accounts of the trial of Jesus, the impression can scarcely be favorable from the point of view of its value as a historical document. Miracles are multiplied, incidents repeated until they fall into groups of three, every occasion is seized to make an event seem the realization of an ancient prophecy.

When we compare it with the other stories, we note that every change by omission or addition of a detail adds an element of improbability. These changes are several times self-contradictory, sometimes they are in conflict with other facts we know, and sometimes they seem rather poor extemporizations. At least we may properly say that is the judgment we should pass on them, if the narrative before us had no pretensions to being a sacred book.

Under these circumstances we cannot treat "John" as a separate source for the life of Jesus. The outline which he uses is before us in the other gospels. There is nothing to indicate the presence of a tradition based on non-extant sources. The most probable account of the composition of "John" would be that he had the very gospels that we have, "Matthew," "Mark," and "Luke," and that his recasting of the story was in the interest of a definite religious movement. There was still in the second and third centuries an attempt to minimize the breach between Christianity and Judaism. "John" seeks to widen it. Peter, whose attitude on this question was opposed to that of the writer and whose traditional authority may have been irksome, is pushed somewhat into the background and made very decidedly inferior to the unnamed disciple who may be intended to be John the son of Zebedee. At any rate, that is one of several conjectures we should have proposed to ourselves, if this story had had no religious association and no traditional sanctity.

In other words, the account of the Passion in the Fourth Gospel is probably the deliberate invention of an imaginative writer. The references to eyewitnesses and other sources would then be examples of established literary technique which pseudepigraphical works of that period frequently show. They cannot be called forgeries because the writers of such books were firmly convinced that historical accuracy in these matters was of far less importance than the end to be achieved—which in this case was a proper conception of the personality of Jesus and his relation to God and to men.

We must distinguish sharply between books like "John" and real forgeries such as those which appeared within the last hundred years in which the purpose of deception is not associated with an intention either to convert or to edify. Examples are the "Essene" letter published in 1847, the letter of "Benan, an Egyptian priest" published in 1910, and finally the "Gospel of Apollonius" published in 1919. All these cite imaginary documents and go through the pretended process of examining them critically. Their fraudulent character is easily enough established.

CHAPTER V

EVALUATION OF THE GOSPEL TESTIMONY

We have accordingly four documentary witnesses about the trial and death of Jesus. Their stories are certainly not alike in detail, and they show strong dissimilarities in general tone and tenor. It may be well to repeat here what was said at the beginning. If these are sacred records, if they are in word and substance the utterance of divine inspiration, their literal truth is our point of departure. Our only task will then be to reconcile their discrepancies as best we may. Of course, it can be done. Apparent contradictions in any books can almost always be reconciled. We must merely be content to use words in unusual and even unprecedented senses. We must assume rather elaborate constructions to fill our gaps. We must, against all probability, recast the statements in other writers to fit the statements here. The result cannot be satisfactory as a plausible historical reconstruction, but that it is a possible feat I should not care to deny.

But that it is possible to do so and to declare the reconciliation a probable one must perforce be denied. And I doubt whether anyone will venture to say that we should even attempt a reconciliation under the postulated conditions —that is, the condition of trying to imagine how we should treat these documents—if they were newly discovered books and if they concerned remote and unrelated situations and persons.

We have already, as it were, cross-examined our witnesses and partially compared them. How shall we sum up their testimony and evaluate it?

First of all, let us recall that instead of four we have really only two stories before us, that of "Mark" and that of "Luke." Whatever changes are made in the story by "John" are, in all probability, arbitrary fictions. They are derived from the writer's pious imagination and not from an independent tradition. Everything in "John" which has even the air of a tradition is also to be found in the other gospels. There is accordingly no reason to suppose that he had any sources which are not before us.

In the case of "Matthew" we may say equally

that there is practically nothing which we can call independent testimony—that is, independent of sources that we have in another form. We could not say this of "Matthew's" Gospel as a whole. There are many parts of "Matthew," not connected with the Passion, which are not found in "Mark" and which do have the look and form of an independent tradition. This source of "Matthew" contains passages of both religious and historical importance. Some of the parables and teachings we most value are to be found here. Whether these things lay before "Matthew" in a complete book or whether he found them as oral traditions we cannot tell. Of one thing, however, we may be fairly sure. He did not invent them, and for many parts of the earlier career of Jesus we cannot ignore them.

But in the story of the Passion, "Matthew" closely follows "Mark," as we have seen, and in all cases but two his changes are minor rationalizations, not greater in extent than we frequently noted in the successive telling of what are meant to be identical stories.

Of the two exceptions one is the story of Judas' repentance and suicide, and the other is the story of Pilate's wife. They are just the type of legends that we should expect to find in the first Christian communities, and while that fact of itself makes it unlikely that "Matthew" invented them, it also makes it highly unlikely that the tradition is based on fact.

The difficulty in the Judas story has already been indicated. No hint is given as to how knowledge of it came to the writer. It is mentioned in no other account. It is impliedly contradicted in the other story of Judas' death found in the Acts of the Apostles (1:23 f.). It is inconsistent and improbable in some of its details. The story of Pilate's wife is equally objectionable. It is awkwardly inserted in the place in which we find it. It belongs to a specific type often found in martyrologies, Jewish, Christian, and pagan, which are very prone to give the persecuting tyrant a compassionate wife or daughter. That it is unhistorical scarcely needs proof. Among other reasons it is highly unlikely that Pilate's wife accompanied her husband. The wives of Roman governors rarely did so, and in later times their presence was distinctly discouraged by the authorities. As a matter of fact, the whole manner and substance of the legend is a trifle grotesque, and we should perhaps be better advised if we took

it as an interpolation which even the completed
form of "Matthew" did not have and which
was inserted by a devout copyist after legends
of the ultimate conversion of Pilate and even
of Caiaphas had become common.

We have then the two accounts to consider,
those of "Mark" and of "Luke." The difference in tone has already been mentioned.
"Mark" is very much concerned to establish
that Jesus was completely innocent of any
crime of which the Jewish court could have
properly convicted him. The accusation that
Jesus declared himself able to destroy and rebuild the Temple he obviously thinks is a serious matter. He is at some pains to show that
no such charge was proved, and though he implies that Jesus was convicted of it, he vehemently asserts that the conviction was unjust.
But that Jesus was in very truth the Messiah,
this much "Mark" certainly believed, and the
answer he ascribed to Jesus on that point is
one that has always given pious commentators
trouble.

For it is impossible to ignore the difference
between the answer Jesus gives to the high
priest and the one he gives Pilate. Except for
our natural reluctance to use epithets like

"evasive" of anything referring to Jesus, I think we should certainly so characterize his reply to the only charge which Pilate brings forward in "Mark's" story, while his answer to the high priest is a bold and unequivocal "I am Messiah!"

In "Luke" the charge of any offense by Jewish law disappears. Nothing is said about the destruction of the Temple or any other "prophecy" which could be declared by an unbelieving court to be directly within the prohibition of Deut. 18:20: "But the prophet which shall presume to speak a word in my name which I have not commanded him to speak . . . . even that prophet shall die." "Luke's" only charges are political, and are specifically stated to be concerned with Roman sovereignty. That there was something in the tradition about "prophesying" appears in "Luke" only in the form of the abuse of Jesus in the high priest's house (22:64–65). Evidently the story was retained as part of the martyrdom when the only thing which gave any point to it—as "Mark" presents it (14:57–60)—was forgotten. This explains why "Luke" completely misplaces the event.

That this difference between "Mark's" ac-

count and "Luke's" is fundamental is, it seems
to me, apparent. It further confirms the greater antiquity of "Mark." When "Luke" was
written recollection of the fact that the Jews
had had a partially autonomous organization
had almost completely disappeared from the
popular mind and was retained only by those
whom we might call the antiquarians and historians, the "doctors" of the schools. "Mark"
—at any rate in its original form—goes back
to a time when this was still a vivid-enough
memory, and when the proceedings before the
national court could not have dropped out of
the story because they must have seemed the
most important of it.

That is to say, there is an apparent reason
why a charge of violating Jewish law may have
been omitted in the story as "Luke" gives it.
There is no apparent reason why it should have
been invented by "Mark."

We may take it then that Jesus was arraigned in the Jewish court on a charge of having violated Jewish law, and such a law as that
contained in Deut. 18:20 may well have been
the specific statute on which the charge was
based.

That this fact appears in so disguised and

mutilated a form in "Luke" is an indication
not only of his later date but also that the persons for whom he wrote would have regarded
Jesus' guilt or innocence as determined by such
a court as a matter of supreme indifference.
Not that the Law of Moses as announced by
Deuteronomy would have seemed so to the
great majority of Christian congregations, but
to those very congregations the overwhelming
conviction of Jesus' divine ministry would
have made a judicial examination of that fact
appear to be preposterous. The action of the
high priest and his Council would be taken to
be merely the expression of Jewish hostility to
Christian doctrine, since few of "Luke's"
readers realized that the Council had ever
possessed a very real authority.

This brings us to the second contrast between "Mark's" story and that of "Luke."
"Mark's" understanding of the organization of
Judea at the time of the death of Jesus is somewhat as follows:

There is a high priest, *archiereus*, and a group
of chief priests, also called by the same name
in the plural, *archiereis*. These persons are
plainly the most powerful of the Jewish community. Besides this there is a Council, *syne-*

drion, which acts as a court, hearing witnesses and issuing formal condemnations. They have a number of attendants, but in no case do these attendants possess military organization or bear military titles. They are a "mob" (*ochlos*).

Over and above this organization is the Roman governor, whom "Mark" calls by the generalized title of *hegemon*. That the governor is the superior of the high priest is obvious enough. But he is not the superior in the sense of being a higher magistrate of the same sort. He is a complete outsider. When the high priest and the Sanhedrin have condemned Jesus, they have exhausted their powers. They surrender him to the other governmental agency which exists in Jerusalem, that of Rome. The term is significant. It is *paredoken*, meaning literally "hand over." The situation is very like that of medieval Europe in which the ecclesiastical court, having condemned a man for heresy, hands him over to the "secular arm"—this secular arm being a series of institutions which might in a pinch refuse to function in spite of the condemnation. The Judean governor, as "Mark" portrays him, had ample discretion in the matter. He may carry out the condemnation or refuse to carry it out. Or he may act independently of it, determining his actions upon charges that have not been investigated before. If, however, he decides to carry out the condemnation, it would make little difference whether it is upon the conviction by the local court or for reasons that seemed adequate to himself.

Now, in "Luke" there is a very significant change. When "Luke" seeks to date the beginning of the ministry of John he does so by calling it "the year when Annas and Caiaphas were high priests." That is to say, he thinks that there could have been two high priests functioning jointly. When the arrest is effected, he says it was done by "the captains of the temple," *strategoi*, implying that there were several.

On these two points "Mark's" statement, as tested by our other sources, is right and "Luke's" is wrong. There was never more than one high priest at a time. The nature of his functions was such that the office could not be held jointly. "Luke" was perhaps misled by the phenomenon of joint magistracy familiar throughout the Roman world and illustrated by the joint consulate at Rome itself. To give the names of the consuls was still the official way of designating the year and must have been known to be so throughout the Mediterranean. Or else "Luke" may have been misled by the double headship of the academy in Jamnia which called itself the Sanhedrin and which, after A.D. 70, gradually became the ecclesiastical Parliament of the Jews—a sort of convocation. In this convocation there had been for many generations a sort of joint primacy enjoyed by two persons, called the *nasi*, or "prince," and the *ab bet-din*, or "father of the court." The names of both were handed down for the times just before and after Jesus as personifying in a measure the academic generation to which they belonged. This would be common knowledge among Jews for several centuries after the destruction of the Temple, and could easily have reached such a person as "Luke" even if his environment was non-Jewish. At any rate, he is wrong about the double high priesthood and "Mark" is right, and since the matter was of no dogmatic importance, the reason must lie in the fact that in the times and surroundings in which "Luke" wrote there was a general ignorance about these matters.

In the same way we must deal with the office of the "captain of the Temple." "Luke" mentions several; "Mark" does not use the term at all. There was such a functionary. Josephus mentions him, using the term *strategos*, just as "Luke" does. But there was only one of them. He was almost certainly identical with the *segan* of the Talmud. He was a civil magistrate subordinate to the high priest, and just as in the case of the high priest, his office was not in fact shared by a colleague and scarcely admitted such sharing. "Luke" therefore has merely a vague knowledge of the existence of an office, but obviously misunderstands it.

That "Mark" does not mention it is easily accounted for. If the arrest of Jesus took place as the two accounts tell it, the high priest determined upon the arrest, sent his servants to seize the accused and have him brought before him. The *strategos epi tou hierou*, the "captain of the Temple," would have had nothing to do with the matter and would not normally take any part in it.

And just as "Luke" knows little of what the political organization of Jerusalem was like, so his version of the hearing before the Sanhedrin bears little resemblance to what we may

suppose must have taken place there as compared with "Mark." We may say that in the
case of both the story of the Sanhedrin trial
must be based on conjecture by their own
showing, but "Mark's" conjecture indicates
a better understanding of what such a tribunal would be likely to do. Jesus in "Mark" is
charged with an offense against Jewish law,
the offense of "false prophecy" for which chapter and verse of the sacred statutes could be
cited. "Mark" is aware that the tribunal
could not act with even a show of legality unless several witnesses appeared for the prosecu-
tion. He also knows that if the testimony is
discrepant, it is valueless. That was not merely
a matter of general sense of fitness but it was
specifically so provided by authoritative ruling.

"Luke" makes the charge before the Sanhedrin and Pilate practically the same. In both
cases Jesus is asked if he is the Messiah. A
claim to be the Messiah—that is, to be king—
was not a charge over which the Sanhedrin had
jurisdiction. It did not constitute an offense in
connection with which direct biblical authority
could be cited. It was, however, an offense
against Roman sovereignty. "Luke" accord-

ingly treats the high priest as if he were exclusively a subordinate Roman official who would act as a committing magistrate to await the judgment of his superior. That certainly was not formally the practice, however closely it sometimes corresponded to the fact under an overbearing governor and a timid high priest.

When in "Luke" we find the further question "Art thou the son of God?" it is only necessary to compare this with "Mark" to see its genesis. In "Mark," after the formal charge of false prophecy is heard and witnesses examined, the high priest asks, "Art thou the Messiah, the son of the Blessed?" As we have seen, "blessed" is here a euphemism for "God." What in "Mark" is one question is made by "Luke" into two, to each of which Jesus answers. That is a situation which is not infrequently found in variants of a common narrative. There is a marked tendency to split an imperfectly understood sentence into two separate ones. And as Jesus' two replies in "Luke" are scarcely responsive at all, while his one reply in "Mark" is decidedly responsive and is a categoric "Yes," we have little difficulty in forming a judgment as to which of these two conjectures implies a clear and vivid pic-

ture of the imagined situation. Plainly it is
"Mark's" and not "Luke's."

The differences in the two accounts concerning the hearing before Pilate depend in a
measure on the way each one conceives the
act of the Council to have been. In the hearing
before Pilate as "Mark" gives it the representatives of the Jews do not take the initia-
tive. Apparently "Mark" supposes the hearing—the only essential hearing—to be over.
Jesus has been tried and condemned—unjustly
condemned, but still condemned. The high
priest delivers him (*paredoke*) to the Roman
governor as a criminal to be summarily dealt
with. It is Pilate who undertakes, on his own
as it were, to investigate the matter.

But "Luke" has a different notion in mind.
In his story there is no real condemnation by
the Sanhedrin whose judicial functions he does
not understand. The high priest holds a sort
of investigation, just the sort that "Luke"
must have seen many a subordinate official
conduct, and having concluded that there is
a case needing the determination of the governor, brings Jesus as an accused, not as a condemned, man before the chief magistrate. And
it is the Jewish representatives who initiate the

proceedings there. They specifically accuse Jesus of sedition and treason.

In both cases the final decision is in the hands of the procurator. In this matter no one living under Roman rule could be in any doubt. Even if we assume that "Mark" had in mind a Sanhedrin and priesthood who could carry out as well as pass a death sentence, it is obvious that nowhere in the *imperium Romanum* could this be done without the consent, express or tacit, of the Roman representative. The differences between the proceedings in the two reports of it incline one to suppose that the trial before the Sanhedrin and the hearing before Pilate formed a single integral story in both versions, since the Pilate account is determined by the view the writer takes of the Sanhedrin trial. Inasmuch as the former is certainly a conjecture, it is likely that the latter is also, a supposition confirmed by considering the general probabilities of the case.

The connection between the two stages of the trial in "Mark" and "Luke" is accordingly determined by the idea each has of the organization of the community. But it is even more determined by the general purpose of the narrative. That purpose in "Mark" is to show the injustice of the condemnation of Jesus by the Jewish court. The jurisdiction of that court is not challenged, but its integrity is. There was no evidence against Jesus on the charges preferred—no evidence which by law should have been considered. The condemnation was therefore unjustified. Pilate's part was secondary. His task was to confirm or disaffirm the court's decree. He would have preferred the latter, as far as his own investigation led him, at any rate, he would have preferred releasing Jesus to releasing Bar-Abbas, but he did not wish to force the matter. Evidently "Mark" takes for granted that normally the sentence would be carried out and that it would need active interposition by the governor to prevent it—at all events, a positive disaffirmance. Pilate is therefore in part made responsible for Jesus' death, but in a lesser degree.

In "Luke" a hazy concept of the functions of the Jewish court compelled all the emphasis to be thrown on the tribunal of the Roman governor. But that went counter to "Luke's" entire conception of Jesus' relation to the Roman state—a conception that was dominant in the Christian community almost from the earliest times, and particularly so in the second century. The Palestinian Jews were rebels against Roman authority. Not so the Christians. That has been one of the striking differences between them even when they had been only slightly differentiated in doctrine and ritual. When, therefore, "Luke" conjectured what could have taken place in such a hearing as that before Pilate, he would hardly have liked to make it seem an instance of Christian suffering at the hands of a Roman oppressor. To a Roman Christian maintaining the contention that Christians had no reason for rancor at Rome, the condemnation of Jesus by Roman authority would not easily present itself as a case in which the Roman authority must be held up to execration.

That is to say, in "Luke's" account in which the Jews appear as accusers and the Romans as judges, it is the accusers' malice rather than the judges' tyranny that would be stressed, and every opportunity taken to relieve the procurator from the main responsibility for the death of Jesus. Evidently, only a weak magistrate could be forced to act against his conviction—as Pilate is represented as doing—but his weakness is venial as compared with the bitter insistence of the "chief priests and scribes."

The two versions of the death of Jesus are therefore far more sharply contrasted in tone and in presuppositions than we might suppose from our habit of deriving a composite account from both of them. Which of the two deserves most confidence? It is hard to refuse assent to the usual view which decides in favor of "Mark." There are many other reasons which make us think in general that "Mark's" Gospel is the older of the two, but the fact that "Mark's" conception of the organization of the community is clear and is right, as far as we can check it, and that of "Luke" is confused and wrong, surely adds a very considerable confirmation to the conclusions to which scholars have long come. Again, not merely the greater antiquity of "Mark" but the difference in the purpose of his writing makes it likely that his account is less colored. His purpose is chiefly apologetic, that of "Luke" is chiefly hostile. We may say, I think, that the latter purpose is more likely to distort an account than the former.

There is only one qualification that we must make. "Luke" gives us the Herod incident which "Mark" omits. Applying the ordinary tests to historical documents like these, we might ask ourselves which is the more likely: that "Mark" omitted it, although the tradition he reported knew it; or that "Luke" added it from other sources, although the dominant tradition did not have it? "Mark" is a very short book. The Herod incident is so far from being an essential matter that the obvious description of it is that it was an unsuccessful attempt on Pilate's part to avoid condemning Jesus. This very fact is however in keeping with "Luke's" general purpose. In other words, we have a reason for "Mark's" omission and "Luke's" retention of what seems to me to be a clear and solid tradition.

That it was the invention of "Luke" or some previous writer with the same pro-Roman and anti-Jewish bias is possible but unlikely. As we shall see, it fits the situation as we know it from external sources so well that it would be a curious coincidence if it were entirely unhistorical. And if we retain the Herod incident, its place can hardly be other than that which "Luke" assigns to it, that is, after the condemnation by the Jewish court and before the execution by the Roman military authorities.

CHAPTER VI

THE ROMAN JUDGE

Are we any nearer than we were before to knowing what took place in Jerusalem during that fateful Passover so many centuries ago when Pontius Pilate was procurator and Tiberius Caesar was lord in Rome? Our two chief witnesses are neither very clear nor particularly convincing. They are not disinterested, and their statements come to us in the form of books copied at least two centuries after they were originally written down, perhaps from copies of copies of that first writing. Only part of what they say is even professedly the statement of eyewitnesses, and even when such direct testimony is asserted, we have no conclusive reason for taking it as such.

And yet, we may claim, I think, that weighing probabilities with probabilities we have at least succeeded in clearing the ground somewhat. That Jesus was tried and condemned by what purported to be the Jerusalem Sanhedrin, that his execution was ordered by the Roman governor, that Herod, the tetrarch of

Galilee, waived any claim he might have over him as sovereign—these, in all probability, are facts, and these facts we must attempt to piece into the picture we can make of the time and place from all possible sources.

A great many of the elements of the picture will also be facts—that is to say, they represent what with a high degree of probability we may assume really to have taken place—and they are facts which have been determined quite independently of the particular picture we are attempting to construct, one concerned with the trial and execution of Jesus. These are the permanent and solid things of our inquiry. But there are other elements in our construction for which we shall have to rely on our imagination. Only the outline of the story is even measurably fixed. Our fancy must fill in the outline.

Obviously that is precisely what the four gospel narrators have done, even the two on whom we found it necessary to rely chiefly: "Mark" and "Luke." But we cannot really compare our effort to theirs, since they had an oral tradition and documents that we no longer possess, and which we therefore cannot evaluate. We may assert, however, that we are doing precisely what "John" did, about whom we may say that he used no documents which we do not possess and that he read the three gospels which precede him in the canon almost—but not quite—in the form in which we read them.

"John" had this decided advantage over us in that he lived in a society much more like that of Jesus' time than ours is. It needs a great effort of the imagination for us to do what he could have done easily, had he been so minded and had he been moved by mere curiosity to discover what the facts were which lay beneath the mass of traditions enveloping the story of Jesus' death.

But the fact is that he was not so minded, and this constitutes the great advantage we have over him. We have not, like him, a specific purpose to serve or a special thesis to establish. And we may utilize the centuries of skilful examination of historical material to teach us methods and warn us of errors—a training which "John" could scarcely have enjoyed even if he had deemed it of value, and we may be sure that he would have regarded it as wholly valueless and despicable.

We may accordingly indulge ourselves in

imagining a series of events in which such persons as Jesus and Pilate and Caiaphas and Herod played parts. The only test by which such a reconstruction must be judged is to inquire whether it is consistent and whether it fits easily into what we know from other sources about the life of the time.

First, we must have some clear notion of the background. These things took place in Jerusalem, an ancient and famous city, and at this time far the most important city of a little Levantine country called Judea. Indeed, to Greeks and Romans the city was really the nation and the country around it little more than outlying territory whose principal function it was to minister to the city's needs. That was not really a correct account of the situation here but it is more nearly correct than any notion that we might transfer from our own conditions to this time. Jerusalem was not quite to Judea what Athens was to Attica, but it was also not what London is to England or Paris to France.

Judea was a frontier province of the Roman Empire. That is to say, in the tremendous system of communities and territories over which the Roman state, the *populus Romanus*, was dominant, the territory of Judea lay at the fringe, at the point where the dominance of Rome ceased. Beyond lay the desert and the group of states belonging to what loosely may be called the Persian, or Parthian, Empire. Being a frontier province, Judea needed a stricter supervision and a closer watching than other provinces required. For that reason the Roman representative—the procurator—was directly responsible to the semi-divine head of the Roman state, the consecrated emperor, *imperator augustus*, in whom the sovereignty of the ruling people was embodied.

Not only was Judea a frontier and a difficult province, but it was inhabited principally by a difficult people, the Jews. The fact that the Jews were scattered throughout the Empire and that the majority of them dwelt outside of Judea would in itself not be exceptional. Much the same was true of Egyptians, Syrians, and of almost every kind of Greeks. But the Jews had an exceptional position because they enjoyed important religious immunities which marked them out and made them a source of embarrassment and disturbance in many of the eastern communities. The Jews in Judea were apparently headstrong, impetuous, and

warlike, notably lacking in cohesion or discipline but with an indomitable pride in their
ancient and unique history and with the recent
recollection of military successes under their
native princes, Simon, Alexander, and Herod.

Added to this was the existence of a powerful
Jewish community outside of the Empire, in
Mesopotamia, a community which by its
wealth and culture exercised a strong influence
on Judea and created there an anti-Roman
faction which co-operated with the nationalistic fanatics.

The Roman world had known peace for
about two generations. There had, to be sure,
been important and dangerous conflicts on the
northern frontier, and fairly continuous guer-
rilla warfare in Spain and Africa. But it was
peace as compared with the generations before
it, and it was the business of the newly created
imperial organization to keep it.

We may see therefore what the problems
were which each successive Roman representative had to face: an open frontier, a turbulent
and difficult people, foreign machinations on
the part of the hereditary enemy, and fanatical
agitation of zealous nationalists. Only eighty
years earlier a Parthian invasion had swept

over Judea. Ten years later the Roman armies
had suffered a most disastrous defeat at the
hands of the same Parthians. Men still remembered all this. Judea was the gateway to
Egypt, which was the granary of the Empire
and the source of much other wealth. For
peace and order the procurator was responsible, and he may well have exhibited a certain
degree of nervousness about it. To maintain
this indispensable peace and order with a
minimum of friction needed tact, military skill,
patience, calmness, profound understanding of
alien peoples, and personal integrity. It will
scarcely be surprising that the average Roman
official fell somewhat short of uniting all these
qualities in his own person. And we know
enough of the Roman governor we are most
interested in—Pontius Pilate (his prenomen is
unknown)—to be fairly sure that he lacked a
great many of them, just as we have a right to
suppose that one of his successors, Gessius
Florus, lacked them all.

What sort of person was this Pilate? Our
picture of him is based in part on widely known
and famous modern paintings and partly on
what we know of men in similar positions at
the present day. Dutch governors in Java,

French governors in Indo-China and North
Africa, but above all English governors in
India, necessarily serve as types upon which
to base our idea of a Roman governor in Palestine. It is curious that we conceive such persons at once as overbearing, haughty, and
somewhat cruel. Obviously, these are not uniformly the characteristics of European governors of Oriental provinces, but the temptation to abuse power is very great in all men
except men of first-rate characters, and it is
especially so when abuse can be rationalized
as extreme anxiety for the interests of one's
own country. Writers like Carlyle and Kipling
demonstrate that there is almost no severity of
provincial repression which will not be en-
thusiastically supported by a cultivated upper
class at home, just as the massacre of Amritsar
in India is still treated by English Tories as
justifiable and necessary. It is consequently
quite natural that some English scholars and
historians have been at pains to defend the
administrations of Pilate and of Florus in
Palestine with the evident consciousness in
their apologies that to condemn Pilate might
lead to unpleasant contemporary applications.

We know of Pilate from Josephus and from

Philo. Both are undeniably hostile, but the point is that there must have been some basis for their hostility. Neither of them is anti-Roman. On the contrary, both are supporters of the Roman system and Josephus is even a fulsome admirer of it. Philo had suffered nothing personally from Pilate. He did not live in Palestine and had never had a reason to fear him. As for Josephus, he was born after Pilate's recall. Neither writer abuses Pilate's predecessor or his immediate successor. Josephus for that matter does not really abuse Pilate. I think we shall have to accept the statement that—at any rate at the beginning of his administration—Pilate was guilty of acts of wanton cruelty, of arrogant abuse of power, and of contemptuous disregard of the rights and sensibilities of at least one of the groups under his jurisdiction, to wit, the Jewish nation occupying the city of Jerusalem and most of the villages and towns of the surrounding hill country, but constituting only a minority in the coast cities and the many other large Greek cities within the territorial range of the procurator's powers.

We must keep in mind what a "procurator" was. We call Pilate the "governor" of Judea,

just as the gospels, even "Mark," call him
hegemon, but there were governors and governors. The title of "procurator" was not a
high one. It was in a sense a creation of the
new system introduced by Augustus. It would
be impossible to set forth here the entire theory of imperial administration as it developed
under Augustus and Tiberius. It must suffice
that the term "procurator" meant an agent in
the strictest sense and was used in private law
as in public with these connotations. The governor proper, the head of a great province, was
the "legatus," the personal representative of
the emperor himself or of the Roman people.
Such a legatus was a senator and generally
himself a part of the governing aristocracy of
Rome. But a procurator's duties were as a
rule sharply circumscribed and in most cases
he had a definite mission.

When a procurator was put in charge of a
territory, just as a legatus might be, it was because the territory was small and because it
had certain special and characteristic features.
Such procurators were given larger powers. Of
one of the procurators of Judea we know that
he had the "power of the sword"—that is the
right to inflict capital punishment—and we

may conjecture that they all had it. When we recall what has been said of the situation of Judea externally and internally, we need scarcely wonder at it.

But even if he had the *ius gladii*, the power of the sword, the procurator was not a man of high position. These positions might be and were filled by imperial freedmen, former slaves. They were quite generally held by former centurions, that is to say, by the class of professional soldiers who rose from the ranks and who were perforce men of courage and bodily strength, but who retained a great deal of the brutality which their training almost necessitated. Above all they were practically never men of intellectual cultivation, and it is absurd to think that the procurator looked upon Oriental provincials as the representative of a high civilization might upon those of a lower civilization. To that extent the famous story of Anatole France, "The Procurator of Judea," gives us a wrong picture.

The striking thing about Pilate's administration of his province was not so much that he was brutally severe but that he was so almost at once and that he seemed to have deliberately undertaken to affront his subjects. There was the affair of the standards. Almost immediately upon assuming his duties in A.D. 26 he marched his troops into Jerusalem with the images of the emperor on the standards unveiled. All previous Roman officials had covered them in order to satisfy the religious objections of the Jews to graven images, particularly in the Holy City. A frantic riot ensued in the course of which a great number of the protestants were killed. Pilate was ultimately compelled to yield.

That he was ignorant of Jewish feeling in the matter or of Roman practice in regard to this Jewish feeling is scarcely admissible. He was no inexperienced subaltern but an old campaigner. It is far more likely that his act was a deliberate provocation meant to justify a severe repression and to establish in a drastic way the tone which the new régime intended to adopt.

Was there any occasion? There is a fact which has not been fully examined but which may explain a great deal in Pilate's conduct of his government during the first years and perhaps may shed a very special light on his later manner. Tiberius succeeded his stepfather in the year A.D. 13. Some years after he selected

Lucius Aelius Seianus—whom we know as Sejanus—as his trusted minister and adviser. Finally in the year A.D. 26 Tiberius, already nearly seventy years of age, retired to the isle of Capri, intending to spend the rest of his life in complete freedom from care or governmental responsibility and leaving Sejanus in complete control of the Empire.

Of Sejanus' personal character or ability it is difficult to form an estimate. Our knowledge of him comes from hostile sources. His power was extremely offensive to the Roman nobility, since he was not of senatorial rank but merely an *eques*, that is, a man of wealth but one who had neither himself held the high magistracies and whose ancestors had held none. His father, however, had been prefect of the praetorians, and later prefect of Egypt, and he himself had taken command of the praetorians on his father's promotion. Apparently, therefore, he belonged to the group of military officials whom the imperial organization was raising into prominence and in whom the emperors confided to the exclusion of the older families.

All the ancient historians of the time describe him as treacherous, vicious, and cruel, and as plotting against his benefactor from the beginning of his rise to power. We may allow

for the evident prejudice of the account but
we can hardly doubt his disloyalty. All his acts
were quite plainly directed to supplanting or
succeeding the aged and morose emperor.

Now, according to Josephus, whom there is
no reason for doubting in this matter, Pilate
was sent to Judea in A.D. 26, the very year in
which Sejanus assumed the virtual headship
of the state. Pilate, therefore, was an appointee and henchman, not of Tiberius but of
his minister, and we may guess that his selection—or better the substitution of Pilate for
Valerius Gratus—had as its primary purpose
the furtherance of the ambitious scheme of the
prefect.

Whether Sejanus was quite the scoundrel the
historians make him out to be may be doubted,
but of one thing we can be sure. He was, for
reasons we do not know, the bitter enemy of
the Jews. The Alexandrian philosopher Philo
wrote a book denouncing his persecutions. If
therefore Pilate was—as seems likely—personally selected by Sejanus for the Judean procu-
ratorship, he must have received direct or implied assurance that the utmost severity would
never want support at Rome. As we have seen,
he lost no time in showing his hand.

As a matter of fact, Sejanus' hostility to the

Jews may have been merely a reflection of his
hostility to the Herodian house which had a
great many connections in Rome. Pilate accordingly presented to the sons of Herod the
same attitude of opposition and suppression
that his immediate chief desired. I think this
explains the massacre of the Galileans at Jerusalem in which he not only established his own
authority but offered a marked and signal in-
sult to Herod's son, the ruler of Galilee, to
whom the offenders should have been referred.
We know that at least four of the Herodian
princes—among whom Herod Antipas of
Galilee may have been included—brought
charges against Pilate at their first opportunity. The acts of Pilate consequently assume
a definite and rational basis if we remember
that his appointment must have been one of
the first acts of the all-powerful vizier.

Sejanus probably had the definite expectation of succeeding or supplanting Tiberius.
The Empire was young. It was not in theory
hereditary. Good fortune, skill, determination,
might bring anyone to the dizzy eminence
which had in relatively recent times been
reached by more than one adventurer. There
was nothing improbable or preposterous in his

ambition. And in its attempted realization we hear of a fact which ought not to be disregarded.

Sejanus had begun to tamper with the army. Doubtless he proceeded with extreme caution. Either directly or through his partisans he had his own images placed on the standards together with those of the emperor. Apparently most of the legions permitted this without objection, or at any rate without effective objection. Only in one place, we are expressly told, did he meet resistance. The Syrian legions refused to add the images of the virtual ruler to those of their sovereign.

But Syria in its general sense included Palestine, and the cohorts under the procurator formed a detachment of these very Syrian legions. We know their names. They were the sixth legion, called Ferrata ("Ironclad"), originally raised by Mark Antony in Syria itself; and the tenth, called Fretensis, whose standards were a bull and a boar. The bull was the abomination of Egypt; the boar, the standing symbol of uncleanness. They were thus especially offensive to the Jewish populace. As originally recruited these legions may have been almost exclusively composed of Romans of Italic stock, but by this time most of the replacements must have been locally selected. These legionaries therefore were to a very large extent Syrians in race and speech, as we are directly informed for the following generation. Under all circumstances they had the reputation of special loyalty and devotion, and their resistance to Sejanus is a special proof of it.

We may guess that Pilate had cautiously assisted in the attempt to win the legions—especially his own troops—for his more immediate chief. If he did, he was probably unsuccessful. At the time his attitude in the matter may have passed without comment, but it cannot have been wholly forgotten.

And then the crash came. What first roused the old emperor's suspicions we are not certain, but his stepson's sudden death and the accumulating opposition to the régime of Sejanus hurried on the catastrophe. Tiberius suddenly returned to Rome. The overwhelmed capital which had yesterday looked upon the all-powerful prefect with cringing terror saw him arrested, summarily tried, and hurried to an ignominious death.

This was in the year A.D. 31. Sejanus' rule had lasted five years. Tiberius held a stringent investigation. A number of the friends and supporters of the minister perished with him.

What was the effect of all this when the news of the minister's fall finally reached the frontiers of the Empire? This might have taken several months, perhaps half a year. One of the first acts of the emperor was to reward the Syrian legions for their loyalty. We may be sure that those who had been in any way close to Sejanus waited with anxious trepidation to see what would happen to them.

Nothing much happened. Tiberius was severe but he was just. He was neither malicious nor vindictive. And he had himself been in command in Syria, and he knew how desperately necessary tranquillity was there. Still, in his headquarters in Caesarea, the procurator of Judea, the appointee of the condemned traitor, must have felt his heart sink more than once in those anxious months of 31 and 32 as he thought of the gloomy old man at Rome, the movement of whose little finger meant life or death, whose natural suspiciousness would make him implacable toward all whom he already distrusted.

Whatever may have been Pilate's conduct when he entered the province, we may be sure that he was not inclined now to give offense anywhere. Sejanus had hated the Jews— doubtless he despised all Syrians—with the arrogant contempt of his kind. Between him and the Herodian princes there seems to have been a personal feud. While Sejanus was at Rome, Pilate could go as far as he wished in his disregard of Judea or Galilee. And indeed the particular acts of oppression and cruelty with which he was charged were all committed in the early years of his administration. There is still another thing we must bear in mind. Pilate was procurator—that is to say, he was an official of inferior rank and restricted juris- diction. But Judea, and indeed all Palestine, was geographically and culturally a part of Syria, although not strictly within the province of that name. Now the governor of Syria was a great man. His headquarters were in Anti- och, the metropolis of the Levant. He was not a mere procurator, but a *legatus Augusti*, "im- perial vicar," commander-in-chief of an army corps, a sort of subemperor. Not only was he a senator but he was regularly an ex-consul, even an ex-censor. While the special position of Palestine necessitated the establishment of an official responsible directly to Rome, the legate at Antioch had a general supervision of the entire region, by virtue of his rank and his great responsibilities. He was the man to whom it was natural to appeal against the procurator, if immediate redress was needed, since Rome was far off, and he might and often did restrain the procurator until Rome could intervene.

Who was legate of Syria in the first five years of Pilate's régime? The titular holder of the office was one of the great nobles, Lucius Aelius Lamia, ex-consul and ex-censor. He had been appointed at some time after A.D. 21— just when we do not know. Normally he would enter on his duties shortly after appointment. But he was never permitted to leave Rome. Tacitus and Suetonius assert that this happened to several of Tiberius' legates, and it may well be so. Still in every case there must have been a particular reason. It was, after all, a rare occurrence. The reason can be conjectured here, if we recall the dates. As early as 21 Sejanus was the sole possessor of Tiberius' confidence. From 26–31, while the emperor was at Capri, Sejanus was sole ruler. If Sejanus' jealousy prevented Lamia from leaving Rome, we should have an adequate

ground for the curious and exceptional fact
that there was no Roman governor in Syria.
And this is partly confirmed by the circumstance that almost immediately after Sejanus'
disgrace and death Lamia was appointed to a
higher position, that of city prefect, the emperor's lieutenant in the capital itself. That
is, in a measure he became Sejanus' successor
as prime minister.

Accordingly, between 26 and 31 Pilate had
not only all-powerful backing at Rome but
had no higher officer anywhere in Syria to control or check him. It is hard to suppose that
this was a coincidence. With the fall of Sejanus
this was changed. The disgrace of his patron
was itself a danger to Pilate, and another thing
had to be considered. He not only lost a sure
protection, but the field was opened to his
enemies, of whom there were many.

The successor of Lamia was the ex-consul,
Lucius Pomponius Flaccus, an intimate friend
of the emperor. Like Lamia, he was of the
highest nobility. He had been governor of
Moesia. Under Augustus he had been of the
group of dissolute nobles in whose society the
poet Ovid learned to his cost that a provincial
rhymester will not be pardoned for doing what

a Roman gentleman might do with impunity. Flaccus reached Antioch about A.D. 32. This was itself ominous, but a greater danger existed in the fact that Flaccus was on friendly terms with the Herodian prince, Agrippa, the darling of the people, grandson of Herod, and in common belief the only legitimate successor to the throne of both Herod and the Maccabees.

This man was essentially an intriguer and adventurer. He had all the advantages of contact with Greek and Roman civilization on its highest levels. He had lived in Rome and in Greece. He was a boon companion of the heir-apparent, Gaius Caesar, the later Emperor Caligula. He was undoubtedly clever and attractive and not overscrupulous. Like all the Herodians, he had been the bitter foe of Pilate. And he remained his enemy. The letter which he wrote to Tiberius, preserved in a fragment of Philo, heaps charges and abuse on the procurator and points to a personal origin of the quarrel between them.

But though he hated Pilate, he hated his kinsmen, the other Herodian princes, as much or more. This was quite normal with the members of that household, especially between the children of different mothers, and indeed it is almost inherent in royal and polygamous courts. Family conspiracy, assassination, and intrigue had ruined the life of the old despot, Herod, who had become the symbol in the East of wealth and power. Agrippa aspired to regain the throne and to make his kingdom as extensive as it had been in his grandfather's time. His uncle Antipas in Galilee was in his way, and he laid plans after the death of Sejanus, their common enemy, to remove him.

He arranged to go to Rome to bring an accusation against his uncle and doubtless one against Pilate at the same time. But he had spent his time in Palestine profitably. He had thrown himself heart and soul on the side of the popular Pharisees and became thereby an open enemy of the governing priestly oligarchy. For that reason he is represented in Talmudic tradition as a virtuous and pious prince, although his right to either designation is more than doubtful.

The procurator must have been fully aware of what was gathering about him. If he had been haughty and overbearing before to all classes of society, we may be sure that he was so no longer. He needed friends. The obvious source was among the other Herodian princes

—the very ones who had signed an accusation
against him before. Above all, the tetrarch of
Galilee, whom he had deeply offended, must
be won over since they both had a common and
dangerous foe in Agrippa.

And equally the "chief priests"—that is to
say, the Judean oligarchy—the enemies of the
Pharisees and of Agrippa, constituted his other
source of support. What his relation had been
with them we do not know. Normally they
were Roman sympathizers, but unless we assume them to have been half-pagan at heart,
Pilate's outrages during the first five years
must have profoundly shocked and alienated
them. Yet it seems that the procurator found
it possible to make his peace with the high
priest Caiaphas and perhaps more than make
his peace. The only hint we have of this renewed understanding is the fact that when in
A.D. 36 Flaccus' successor, Lucius Vitellius,
interfered in Judea and sent Pilate under arrest to Rome, he dismissed Caiaphas as well,
although he had been high priest for fifteen
years, and appointed Ananel as his successor.

We need not be surprised at Pilate's success-
ful diplomacy. The picture of the Roman,
straightforward if ruthless, whose empire was

built on energetic military conquest is wholly inadequate. The Romans were if anything as adroit in their diplomacy as they were success-ful in their battles. Indeed, it has often seemed that they owed their dominance rather to the former than to the latter quality. Even an ex-centurion would know how to be supple when he found it necessary.

We must therefore seek to rid our minds of the conventional picture of Pontius Pilate in the year A.D. 33, shortly after the death of Sejanus. He was not the haggard and stern proconsul who represented Roman and Greek civilization amid a motley crew of noisy and repulsive Orientals, upon whom he gazed with at best a shrug of contemptuous indifference. He was a minor official, very nervous and very uncertain of his own position, eager to make friends and placate former foes, very eager in-deed to give no further handle to the enemies who were waiting for their chance to pounce upon him. We may even guess that the crea-ture of Sejanus whom the Syrian legions had refused to flatter—an act for which they had just been decorated—was not overpopular with his soldiers.

How would such a man have acted in the

events which related to Jesus? His headquarters were usually at Caesarea, Herod's
magnificent city on the coast, some forty miles
northwest of Jerusalem. But on the great pilgrimages when hundreds of thousands of men,
Jews and Gentiles, streamed to the Zion hill,
he naturally moved to the capital. Pilgrimages
of this sort were inevitably dangerous. The
very crowds created a danger, even if they had
been exclusively pious and harmless devotees.
But that is what most of them were not. From
Cyrene, from Egypt, from Galilee, from Syria,
and from Asia Minor there poured in the weeks
before Passover a mixed multitude, all in a
certain state of excitement, many of them rude
and passionate, many of them violent and
quarrelsome. And there can be no doubt that
besides the pilgrims proper an indefinite number of people of all descriptions fastened themselves on the pilgrim trains with more sordid
desires than those of worship. We may be sure
that in those weeks the cohorts encamped in
Jerusalem slept under arms and that every
little tumult might become a riot.

If therefore on the morning of one of the
days of the Passover feast a Galilean was
brought bound to his tribunal with the report

from the high priest that he had been duly
condemned of a capital crime by the Jerusalem
court, what can the procurator have thought?
The account of "Mark" fits so well into what
we have independently found to be the background that we can accept it as true in outline,
although it can scarcely be so in detail. That
Pilate would conduct a lengthy examination
is highly improbable. A request from Caiaphas
with the assurance that all due forms had been
observed would ordinarily be carried out as a
matter of course. But there were two difficulties.

First of all, Pilate desired no disturbances.
It can scarcely have been unknown to the
masses that Sejanus was dead and that the
legate at Antioch was a friend of the popular
Agrippa. This Jesus delivered to him for execution, who and what was he? The high priest's
message itself indicated that he was a trouble-
maker of some sort. He was further charged
with having assumed the title of "king." But
if he was all this, he must have a following.
Would there be an attempted jail-delivery?
Would his execution provoke a riot? It was
well to proceed warily.

Pilate was further troubled by Bar-Abbas.

Historians and critics have wondered why if Bar-Abbas was a rebel taken in arms, he was not at once hanged. The reason is probably simple enough. If he was an insurrecto-chief his men probably thronged the streets. While the feast was on Pilate had not dared to execute him. We can see that if Jesus was also a popular leader the thought might have occurred to him that he could execute the more dangerous man and pardon the other. Caiaphas might be offended but an outbreak was just now more serious than the high priest's anger.

And added to all this, Jesus was a Galilean, and the tetrarch was in Jerusalem for the Passover. If Pilate had previously offended Herod, here was a chance to extend the olive branch. And he had every reason to believe, as was the fact, that Herod was as desirous as he for a reconciliation.

It is even possible that another thought came to the procurator's mind. He could in a way secure these results simultaneously. He would gain Herod's friendship, and he would avoid a popular demonstration. And he did not after all have to break with Caiaphas, for he could show that he was under a duty to surrender the man. Besides, the priests and the

Herodians were generally on good terms and Herod would probably send Jesus to Galilee and there execute him.

Evidently he miscalculated. Herod was willing to be friends, but he did not care to incur additional odium. Five years ago he had executed the popular Baptist. Echoes still lingered of that, since John's disciples formed a sect. Courtesy for courtesy, he sent Jesus back and waived his rights.

It is likely enough that the rest was routine. Perhaps Pilate did not even see Jesus when he was brought back from Herod—a proceeding which may have taken a day or more. The man had already been condemned. His execution had been suspended: first, long enough to discover that whatever following he had was not likely to be dangerous; and, second, out of deference to Herod. When Herod waived his rights, Jesus was delivered to some sergeant who already had a batch of prisoners designated for crucifixion, several poor wretches— we cannot be sure that they were two in spite of the gospel account—condemned for a theft which may have been petty enough in our estimate.

The clever story of Anatole France, "The

Procurator of Judea," must therefore be qualified as to the picture it draws of Pilate. Whether Pilate did or did not remember Jesus shortly after his execution we cannot be sure. Even if he did not remember his name, he may have remembered that a Galilean had been executed during that spring pilgrimage of 33 and had given him an occasion for gaining the friendship of the tetrarch of Galilee.

We have tried to approach the position of Pilate at the trial of Jesus with no other aid than that gained from the sources themselves, and it has seemed that in this way it becomes somewhat more intelligible. But all the while we have been assuming a fact about which the sources really leave us quite in the lurch, and, that is the exact year of Jesus' death.

What may be called the older traditional view put it in A.D. 33. That year, however, was fixed by a sixth-century monk, Dionysius the Little, who arbitrarily assumed that the ministry of Jesus began a year later than John's and who took the "about thirty years" of Luke 3:23 as a precise figure. Other pious commentators, ancient and modern, relying on the story of the Magi and the Massacre of the Innocents, have found it necessary to put the birth of Jesus in 4 B.C., the year of Herod's death. That would give us 29 or 30 for the year of his death, provided we take the "about thirty" as Dionysius did and assume that, as "John" guessed, the ministry of Jesus lasted just three years.

Obviously the story of the Magi is a miraculous legend which can hardly be taken to be probable, and the Massacre of the Innocents, while not miraculous, is also a legend of which we shall have to say that it is very unlikely. And certainly it is clear that those who base the date of Jesus' birth or death on these events begin with the assumption that the stories are true because they are in the gospels and have not investigated them as they would have investigated similar stories about other events.

Since we have decided to go about it differently, we can hardly do better than go back to the one date in the gospels which is given with something like precision, the date of John's first appearance as a preacher (Luke 3:1). "Luke" has evidently taken pains with it and has checked it twice, as we have had occasion to notice before (p. 110). The date he gives is the fourteenth year of Tiberius which we are today in an even better position to be sure about than historians were a generation ago. It must be A.D. 28–29. Jesus was associated with John, left him and preached independently, acquired a reputation and a following, went to Jerusalem on a Passover pilgrimage, and was there seized and put to death—and all this must have happened in the years after A.D. 28.

How long after? The "three years" of John form a sacred number to which we can hardly attach serious historical value. The assumption that all these things took place in one year is difficult to accept, and it does not become less difficult because second- and third-century Christians did not find it so. To them, indeed, the suddenness and briefness of such a career for Jesus was all the easier to credit because it seemed miraculous.

Modern critics and scholars have painstakingly investigated matters as difficult as the local Jewish calendar and as remote as astronomical calculations of eclipses in order to determine the exact year of Jesus' death. What seems to me to make these calculations useless for our purposes is that they always depend on particular statements in the gospels which are themselves rather vague or of more than doubtful probability.

We are then thrown back again to the spring of the year A.D. 28 as our earliest date, and we can only say that at some time after that the trial and death of Jesus took place. If it was more than three years after, it came after the fall of Sejanus, and the attitude of Pilate, as it has seemed possible to reconstruct it in the previous pages, takes on a particular coloring. Weighing probability with probability, we are surely not overtaxing likelihood when we say that three years is not a long time for John's fame to have resounded through Galilee, for Jesus to have joined him and to have withdrawn from him in order to preach his own gospel, for John to have been executed, and for Jesus' personal renown as a healer and preacher to have spread through Galilee and Judea and to have excited enthusiastic veneration and aroused official apprehension. It might have taken much longer, but if it were more than three, four, five, or six years, it would still give us the picture of Pilate we have tried to draw.

CHAPTER VII

THE JEWISH COURT

At the time that Jesus was tried the Jews occupied a position in the world quite different from the two situations in which we are likely to imagine them. Of these two, one is the position of the Jews throughout the Middle Ages in Christian Europe. It was one of scarcely qualified outlawry. Jews were not legally members of any civic community in which they lived and could be ejected at will. The second is the present position of Jews in the same countries as well as in America. In most of these countries the legal condition of Jews does not differ from that of other citizens. Neither disability nor privilege is based upon the fact of Judaism. None the less, in these same communities the Jews for the most part live in groups which only exceptionally mingle with non-Jewish groups.

The Jews at the beginning of the Christian Era were neither outlaws nor were they legally indistinguishable from the rest of the inhabitants of the Empire—and this Empire was, as we cannot say too often, not an organized single state or superstate, but merely the fact that within a large number of related communities of all kinds the Roman state was the dominant and responsible guarantor of peace. The Jews lived all over the Mediterranean, but more than seven-eighths lived in the eastern half. We shall do well to remember that they formed a far greater fraction of the total population than is now the case.

Now, in most parts of the Empire, the Jews lived as members of various civic communities, but generally their membership was not the same as that of other groups. This was not in itself surprising since there were a great many grades and degrees of citizenship, and many other groups corporately organized had privileges and duties dependent on such organization. The Jews in most of the cities of Asia, Syria, Cyprus, Africa, and Egypt were corporately organized, and while their privileges were often peculiarly irksome to the local authorities, their position differed only by slight gradations from that of other corporations.

But in Palestine, within what had been the limits of an independent kingdom from about 130 to 63 B.C. and a vassal kingdom from 63 to

3 B.C., the situation of the Jews was different. Here also there was a number of small and great civic communities in which Jews lived in varying numbers, as they lived in the cities of Asia and Syria. But there were, besides, several small principalities, in each of which the entire body of Jews and some non-Jews were indistinguishably gathered as a loosely organized "nation." One of these was Galilee, around the lake of that name; another was Iturea; a third was Judea, including Idumea to the south.

In Judea there was the further complication that the native prince had been dismissed. But the "nation" did not thereby completely lose its autonomy. The place of the prince— Herod's son Archelaus—was taken by an oligarchy, reverting in this way to the governmental organization which had prevailed in Judea from the return to the Maccabean revolt.

Those who composed that oligarchy were, first of all, certain clans of the hereditary priestly caste. These priests had in Old Testament times held something of the positions of the Brahmans of India or the priests of Egypt, but they had never exercised anything like the authority these castes had enjoyed. After the return, however—from about 500 B.C. on—some of the priestly families gained in power and influence to such an extent that it was among them only that the high priest was selected. Under the Greek suzerains of Syria and Egypt the high priest became a virtual monarch and the high-priestly clans a close oligarchy of nobles. Below them were the ordinary priests, then the subordinate class of Temple ministrants, the Levites, and outside of these, the great mass, the plebs.

But both priests and people were intersected by many parties or sects, the two terms being more alike than we ordinarily suppose. Parties and sects had sprung up in profusion during the Greek dominance, and the two most marked divisions, the Hellenizers and the nationalists, developed a mutual and bitter hostility. A nationalist movement resulted in 164 B.C. in a war for independence which gave the Hasmonean family both the high priesthood and the throne, although the Hasmoneans were not, properly speaking, of the high-priestly clans at all, but an obscure rural branch of one of the lower priestly families.

In the period of prosperity and conquest

which followed Hellenizers ceased to be an organized party but the term remained a general attitude which might be found in all classes in different degrees. New parties appear which in many instances assumed the form of corporate organizations. All over the Roman world religious and half-religious corporations abounded. It was a simple and natural thing for those who professed common interests, whether in doctrine or economic pursuits or merely in games, to form an association very much in the modern fashion, with officials, with stated meetings, and with a certain amount of common property. And it was just as usual for these local societies to be united in a loose federation if the common purposes transcended local bounds.

So we shall understand the "sects" which sprang up in Palestine under the native kings, in the concrete form of corporations or guilds or conventicles, many of them using the Greek word "synagogue" or "congregation" to express the fact of their organization, but adding to that word the name of the group itself or the name of their leader or chief. It was therefore not the building which was so called but the association. In any town of Palestine there

was no "synagogue" as such, corresponding to
the parish church of the Middle Ages, but
there might be a "synagogue of Pharisees," "a
synagogue of Sadducees," "a synagogue of
disciples of John," and so on. In many places
one group alone may have been important. In
others there might be half-a-dozen Pharisaic
synagogues.

Of these sects we know the names of three:
the Pharisees, the Sadducees, and the Essenes.
But there certainly were a great many more.
It is likely that most of them lasted only a
short time, during the life or perhaps during
the vogue of some leader. And evidently a great
many persons belonged to none of them, whatever their leanings or sympathies might be.

Again, there were guilds—the same type of
guild as those which we find all over the Roman world, guilds of artisans—fullers, tanners,
potters, musicians. These, too, were corporately organized. There was nothing to prevent
a man from belonging to several corporations,
and nothing to prevent a guild from adopting
some official religious doctrine or ceremonial
as the basis for its organization.

One of these guilds we must particularly
mention because of its special rank in the

community. This was the guild of Sopherim,
or "scribes." Originally they seem to have
been the men who copied the ancient Scriptures and were therefore expert in them. They
must have soon become the particular experts
in the sacred language, Hebrew, which had
ceased since the return to be the language of
everyday intercourse. They were probably in
great demand as teachers and in special demand in the various synagogues for the purpose of expounding and translating the books
which had by the time of Jesus decidedly become holy books.

Echoes of the controversies of the sects have
come down to us in several books, the gospels
themselves being one of our sources of information. Up to the time of the dissolution of the
"nation of the Jews" as a definite entity—
which took place after the last great insurrection under Simeon bar-Kosiba in A.D. 133—
the Pharisees had been growing in influence
among the masses, but the governing nobility
had been largely Sadducee. The special functions of that nobility, their priestly duties, had
ceased with the destruction of the Temple in
A.D. 70. But they still retained the prestige of
their former dominance, and they continued to

exercise in Judea whatever local and municipal authority was not gathered into the hands of the constantly increasing corps of Roman officials. In the reconstituted Sanhedrin at Jamnia, become now a religious convocation rather than a senate, the number of Pharisees multiplied. They must have been a majority before the revolt, and shortly afterward the Sadducees dwindle and disappear.

In A.D. 33, however, the Pharisees were far from this position. Probably a majority of the people were Pharisee, but the priests and the Council most decidedly were not. The Talmud—even its basic text, the Mishna—is before us only a Pharisaic redaction of A.D. 200, and when the older teachers are depicted as the exponents of what was to become Pharisaic orthodoxy, we must remember that for many generations the Pharisees were in the eyes of the then orthodox a sect of dangerous and subversive heretics.

It is likely that the especial warders of that older orthodoxy were the scribes and that most of the scribes were Sadducees. At any rate, the position of the Sadducees was that of an uncompromising and rigid adherence to the revealed law, without expansion or interpretation by tradition and with an especially determined rejection of those newer beliefs which had spread so widely and which the Pharisees had embraced so eagerly. The foremost of these doctrines was the belief in the world-to-come—the belief in a personal immortality of happiness for the elect, and the elect were obviously the members of the Pharisaic congregations, who formed a brotherhood, just as the Pythagoreans did in Italy, and who called themselves "comrades."

Whether this immortality was to begin immediately after death or after a world-cataclysm, followed by a Resurrection of the comrades, is not quite clear. It is likely that opinions differed from synagogue to synagogue and from comrade to comrade. The Resurrection, however, was a prominent dogma of the Pharisees and a special issue between them and their rivals.

Of Pharisee practices, as distinct from their dogmas, we know several which struck their contemporaries. They baptized their neophytes, they vigorously proselytized among Jews and Gentiles, and they justified their innovations by assigning great authority to oral tradition.

The world-to-come doctrine, which played so prominent a part in pharisaic beliefs, was a great religious movement which far transcended Palestine and had perhaps originated centuries earlier in Asia Minor or Thrace. It had a profound appeal for the great mass of the people, slaves and semislaves as most of them were, or else peasants ground by tax-collectors and plundered by armies and marauders. Everywhere it took various forms, and in Palestine not only Pharisees but other groups, temporary or permanent, announced the same promise with exciting enthusiasm.

And, as is usual in such matters, the gathering excitement dramatized and accelerated the conditions so ardently desired. What was a vague and infinitely remote prospect, dependent on cycles of metamorphoses and purgatories, became in each new preaching a nearer and more readily attainable goal. The world, this world, must first go up in flames. Granted, but it will happen sooner than was supposed. And thousands yearned to believe that it was imminent.

The prevailing eschatology—which long word merely describes the belief in the coming of the Last Day—was strongly inclined to shorten

the time of its arrival, and throughout Palestine, especially in Galilee, a little removed
from the direct influence of priests and Sadducees and scribes, men appeared to declare
that it was at hand. This was the "evangel,"
the "good news," but it was an evangel because the last day of this world was the first
of the world-to-come, the permanent and ever-
lasting Kingdom of Heaven. Evidently only
the elect, the saints, the comrades, the initiates
—or whatever names the sects gave themselves
—would be citizens of this state. What would
happen to the rest, to the "people of this
world," the *am ha-aretz*, was not always specified. Apparently, in Pharisaic doctrine they
would simply not be. Of an infinity of suffering
there is no suggestion.

Classes of citizens—synagogues of sectaries
—these do not exhaust the description of the
people. There was another movement which
traversed all classes and might be found in all
congregations. Men were nationalists in various degrees and anti-nationalists.

Nationalist agitation had existed in Palestine for a long while—certainly since the beginning of the second century B.C. A handful
of fanatics had at that time offered resistance

to the Greeks and suffered martyrdom. Stirred
by their example, the sons of Hasmonai had
risen in revolt against the great King Antiochus, had routed his armies, dispossessed a
disloyal priesthood, and established an independent state. The state was still there in
A.D. 33, but the independence was gone and
there was no corner of Palestine in which some
men did not passionately resent the presence
of the Romans and their indisputable sovereignty in a place where only God and his annointed ought to bear rule.

We shall have to concern ourselves with this
annointed of God. The world-to-come was a
dream all over the earth, but in this corner of
the earth it was fused with another doctrine.
In the land which had once been David's,
there was only one lawful and legitimate rule,
and that was the rule of a king of David's
blood, annointed by God,—and therefore Messiah—and guided by his prophets. When this
notion took this particular form we cannot be
sure. But in all its forms the messianic idea
was from the first associated in a definite way
with the picture of the Last Day and the coming Kingdom of God. The Maccabeans were
not of Davidic line, and we are expressly told

in contemporary records that their rule was legitimate only as a preparation—until a "trustworthy prophet" should arise to announce the Messiah.

As is usual in such cases, the expectation of the Messiah increased just when to sober outsiders the prospects of independence dwindled more and more under the slowly tightening rule of Rome. In teeming Galilee particularly, in direct proportion to the relatively lower state of culture, preachers and agitators arose one after another with claims widely varying in extent. Some claimed to be the Messiah, others the precursor of the Messiah, the "trustworthy prophet" of the Book of Maccabees. To popular imagination this prophet easily became individualized as Elijah, the most powerful and dramatic figure among the ancient mouthpieces of the Lord. Most of these men were undoubtedly sincere just as were most of the miracle-workers, oracles, thaumaturges, who sprang up everywhere, but in both classes there must have been a fair sprinkling of frauds and quacks. Besides, nationalism and even messianism were the easiest pretexts under which marauders challenged Roman authority or any authority. Again the Parthians, the hereditary enemy across the Syrian Desert, in one way or other gave secret and open support to anything which imperiled or weakened Roman power in the land which was so easily considered within the Parthian sphere of influence.

In this way nationalism, love of liberty, religious beliefs, and a passionate hope of immortality were welded into a moving and seething mass that needed all the wits of wise men to control, if so be it could be controlled at all.

This is the glimpse we get of Palestine after an interval of some nineteen centuries. How did it appear at the time to the Roman officials or to the priestly nobles? As far as the Romans were concerned, the answer is obvious enough. Even to a tolerant or half-sympathetic Roman —and there were doubtless such men—the prevailing eschatology and the messianic idea, translated into terms he could understand, could only have meant some such thing as the following. First there was to be a general crashing of existing institutions and then the reign of a sovereign, the God-annointed king at Jerusalem, immensely superior to the Roman imperator and wholly supplanting him.

Plainly, to any Roman eschatology meant anarchy and messianism meant treason, and the spread of both of these ideas meant imminent peril at one of the danger spots of the Empire.

Whatever savored of these things we know the Roman officials suppressed with prompt and ruthless severity. It was fortunate for the procurators of Judea that most of this was centered in Galilee and not in Judea itself. For Galilee, Herod Antipas was responsible. It was evident that Herod was a little weak, a little lax, and it was evident too that it might become necessary to relieve him, as his brother Archelaus had been relieved. But for the present the time of greatest anxiety for the procurators was the seasons of the great pilgrimages —the spring (Passover), the harvest (Pentecost), and the autumn (Tabernacles). Unless care was taken, it was almost inevitable that in the stream of people hastening to the Zion hill there would be countless agitators and rebels, fanatics and adventurers, and that any riot might be the prelude to a revolt.

If this was the Roman attitude, that of the priestly oligarchy must have been the same. In the days of the Greek domination the upper ranks of the priesthood had been outright

Hellenizers, frank apostates, and assimilators, eager to abolish barbarous rites and customs and language in order to become Greeks in the fullest sense. This was no longer the case two centuries later. The priests were cosmopolitan in culture and many of them Greek in speech, but they were none the less Jews in observance. Indeed their privileged rank rested on the permanence of the Jewish ritual. Nor must we forget that their prosperity was largely derived from the control of the Temple and its considerable resources. To them the Roman rule meant security, and nothing else gave even the remotest promise of such security. The nationalism of most Pharisees was therefore as objectionable to them as pharisaic doctrines were abhorrent, and the rise of every new Messiah seemed to threaten them far more than it seriously imperiled Roman dominion.

There is an interesting modern parallel in the situation at present in India. Whatever strength the movement for independence may have in the country at large, native princes who rule over one-third of the Indian Empire are almost unanimously supporters of British rule, many of them in the honest fear of the anarchy which the withdrawal of that rule might produce and some because it permits them to exploit their own lands with impunity. So, in Judea, besides priests who saw in Rome the only guaranty of peace, there were some who used Roman partisanship as a cover for rapacity, whose religion was indolence or pretense and who may have been deterred from open paganism only by fear of their fellow-Jews.

In any case, the oligarchy knew that during the pilgrimages the standing menace of nationalism was intensified. Not only was the occasion one of superheated feeling at high tension, but the presence of great crowds gave an illusion of strength and power, and excited and ignorant men might forget how great, how persistent, and how deadly in her wrath was the distant city represented to their eyes by a handful of legionaries.

Of the many preachers and agitators, founders of new corporations, proclaimers of new doctrines, the authorities—both Jewish and Roman—were aware only of some. The Romans would be interested in those whose political attitude was clearly hostile—those who could be called rebels and suppressed, or who could be denominated bandits and hunted down. In the mountains and desert it was not always easy to be certain whether a gathering of armed men denoted marauders seeking plunder or zealots attempting to cast off the foreign yoke. When these things occurred in Judea the procurator acted promptly. When they occurred in Galilee, he, as well as the legate at Antioch, could only hope that Herod would deal with the situation as briskly as his father would have done—a hope often enough frustrated.

But the "chief priests," while concerned enough with open nationalistic outbreaks, were also even more interested in the religious movements which directly threatened them and indirectly endangered the Roman hegemony. Echoes of such movements came often enough. They must have heard of John whose preaching had drawn men from all Palestine, and they must have waited with impatience to see how long Herod would endure the noisy disturbance of this half-mad sectary. For, not only did John preach anarchy—what else was the imminent Kingdom of Heaven but anarchy?—but he was obviously political. His politics kept this side of nationalism, but if he denounced Herod, the friend of Rome, one could not tell what he might denounce next. Doubtless Caiaphas at Jerusalem and most respectable and solid citizens breathed more easily when news came that Herod had seized and executed John.

Doubtless just as they heard of John, so after John's death they heard of Jesus, a carpenter of a petty village in Galilee, who preached the end of the world and the coming Kingdom with great fervor and success. Like John and the Pharisees he baptized; and like them both he preached the Resurrection in the flesh; but unlike them both he avoided politics. It may be for that reason that the indolent tetrarch, his lord, regarded him as a harmless zealot and let him alone.

But to the chief priests he was not harmless. He proclaimed the approaching Kingdom of Heaven as so close upon the world that the clinging to family and property was ludicrously futile. All ties were to be dissolved at once, all obligations cast aside, all ordinary human hopes and desires spurned, in the overwhelming eagerness to possess a share in the world-to-come, which was so soon and so visibly to be realized. The miracles of healing with which

he was credited made educated men shrug
their shoulders. He might have seemed even
to nervous oligarchs merely an absurdly fan-
tastic mountebank, if the ominous story had
not begun to spread that he was a prophet—
John risen from the dead, Elijah the precursor
of the Messiah—the Messiah himself. Joseph
Caiaphas, the high priest, must have devoutly
hoped that he would not take it into his head
to come to Jerusalem in any of the great pilgrimages.

His fears were realized. In the twenty-first
year of Tiberius Caesar he arrived for the
Passover with a small band of followers, mostly Galileans. His preaching doubtless drew
crowds, as anyone's preaching might have
done, but to the watchful priests the crowds
that followed Jesus were exceptionally large,
or else exceptionally persistent.

What moved them to take action? Wild
words were reported to them, extravagant
statements heard and credited, acclamations
that could readily be called treason. Jesus
preached quietism and in worldly matters indifference, but his intense spirit was in apparent contradiction with non-resistance. Certainly, if his denunciations were frequent and

violent, he would have seemed all the more a true successor to Amos and Isaiah, and lordly gentlemen sitting on silken couches heard with no feigned resentment and dread the beggarly Galilean deny to rich and powerful and wise any share in the community of saints.

Perhaps, as the feast drew nearer, there were minor tumults. Josephus tells us how often they took place. Rumors were about that the procurator was not so firm in his seat of authority. The people's prince, the half-Maccabee Agrippa, was on his way to Rome to get tardy satisfaction against the brutal Pilate and his crony, the arrogant high priest. Hotheads may have scoffed at the Roman standards. In the crowds in the squares there were rough men enough, unemployed soldiers, hard-living herdsmen from the desert. It needed little to make a brawl seem a riot.

Little of this could be directly traced to the preaching of Jesus, but the high priest and his friends would need no direct evidence. If he had said only a tithe of the things credited to him it was enough to make an indictment.

Perhaps the high priest urged the procurator to act directly. The messianic claims put forth by Jesus' followers might well have seemed to justify Roman intervention. In that case we may suppose that Pilate declined to incur additional odium at this stage in his own fortunes. There had been no overt act. If the Jerusalem authorities wished to deal with this fellow according to their own law, that was their affair.

But on the whole it is more likely, just as "Mark" tells the story, that the high priest acted without reference to the procurator. The man was to be stopped and the high priest ordered his arrest. It cannot have been easy to find him, and if an open search had been made, it might have proved dangerous—non-resistant as the new doctrine was. According to the Judas legend, as "Mark" reports it, the task of the priests was made easy by the treason of one of Jesus' disciples. This may literally have been the case. Bickerings and quarrels existed in the very earliest Christian community after Jesus' death. There may have been such quarrels in his lifetime. And if hot-tempered men quarrel, violent acts of vengeance or betrayal are done often enough before their blood has cooled.

Or else the Judas story is a novelized version of a split that occurred among Jesus' adherents, involving the withdrawal of Judas and perhaps others with him. When the arrest took place, the natural suspicion would at once arise that the seceders had betrayed their former leader, and we may be sure no careful or dispassionate investigation would be held to determine whether it was in fact so.

We are, most of us, familiar with the procedure in criminal investigations. The accused person is arrested, arraigned before a committing magistrate, specifically accused, and formally tried. He may, and he generally does, appeal to a higher court, if he is convicted. All these things take time, and there is almost necessarily an interval of weeks and months between the later stages of the procedure. But above all the procedure is strictly regulated by law, and any serious deviation is not merely an irregularity but will probably prevent punishment from being inflicted.

Ancient criminal law was also regulated and in some respects very precisely. The regulations were not always intended to safeguard the rights of the accused but were in large part based upon the fact that most procedure, civil as well as criminal, was a form of ritual, and was particularly ritualistic when matters of life and citizenship were involved. But the sanction was quite different. There was rarely an appeal based on error in the court below, and it is only exceptionally—as at Rome—that the judgment of a court could be prevented before it was carried out. Usually appeals were appeals to the mercy or clemency of a monarch or of a popular assembly, and a judge or other officer who defied the regular procedure could be held to account after his act but not before it.

In Judea we do not know the procedure during the centuries immediately before and immediately after the birth of Christ so well as we know the Roman and Greek procedure of that time. We have the two main sources of information, Josephus and the Talmud. The Talmud is far more complete and systematic, but it was written down somewhat later and its statements are those of patriotic antiquarians. There is a strong tendency to magnify the functions of the court, to surround it with grandeur and solemnity. The talmudic account is subject to the further qualification that it was made by a sect which at the time that concerns us was in active opposition to those who actually administered the government and the courts. We must suppose that the Talmud often tells us rather how third-century scholars thought they would have acted than how in A.D. 33 the law was actually enforced.

But there are certain things we can regard as highly probable. There was in Jerusalem a body of which we have often spoken, the Sanhedrin. This word is a Hebraized form of a Greek word, *synedrion*, and therefore shows us at the same time whence it was derived and how completely it was adopted. The Sanhedrin, or Council, corresponded to the Greek *bulē*, or the Roman Senate. It was in origin an advisory body, and in most parts of the Mediterranean it had become to a greater or less degree the governing corporation of the state. Evidently in oligarchies that would inevitably be the case, and it was so in Judea.

In theory the Sanhedrin consisted of seventy men, exclusive of its presiding officer. Seventy was a holy number and was doubtless selected for that reason. That there were always seventy in office seems highly improbable, if we consider what took place elsewhere. Seventy was probably merely a maximum number. Their functions were primarily political even under a Roman procurator, and since there is no indication that there was anything like a popular assemblage, their decrees would have the force of laws—in fact, only their decrees would have such force.

The chief magistrate of the state—whatever his title—always retained a certain amount of summary jurisdiction in all the states of the Mediterranean. He almost always had the power to punish offenses committed in his presence and in defiance of him. But for most crimes there was a systematic way of going about it and it regularly involved a public tribunal—that is, a tribunal which either actually was, or by a fiction could be supposed to be, the popular assembly itself, since governmental and judicial functions were never completely separated. Where there was no popular assembly, the Council held or usurped those powers.

Apparently that had been done in Judea where the Sanhedrin was the only court. Who were the members and how were they selected? The second question can be answered most easily. They were appointed by the king while there was one; by the high priest when there was no king. The other possible methods, election to existing vacancies by the Council itself,

popular ballot, hereditary succession, are almost surely excluded by all we know of local
conditions. This appointment, however, was
not completely free. There was a certain number of families which, as we have seen, constituted at this time a hereditary nobility.
The heads of these families could not be passed
over, and there is every likelihood that for a
long time they formed the majority.

The minority were selected from those men
in the community who for one reason or another had become distinguished. Wealth must
have played some part, but a far greater part
was played by reputation for "wisdom." This
wisdom was specifically a knowledge of the
Sacred Scriptures and a capacity of applying
it by interpretation and homily. Surely many
of the guild of scribes were also members of
the Council, and it had never been feasible
to ignore completely the popular and heretic Pharisees. Indeed, it is possible that the
"wise men" who were members of the Council
were nearly all Pharisees, since the other groups
would be described more specifically as priests
and scribes. In the later days of Pharisee
domination the phrase "the wise" was the
ordinary way of indicating the majority of

the Sanhedrin. While, therefore, the Council members were the appointees of the chief magistrate, whether king or high priest, in fact the high priest's freedom of selection—and perhaps the king's—was limited in the way indicated. The high priest would see to it that the Sanhedrin had a majority of his class, i.e., of priests. Under King Agrippa, shortly after, an increasing number of "the wise" were probably selected.

In any case, we must suppose the councilors to be oldish men, fifty or over, most of them much older. They were probably all residents of Jerusalem, although many probably had estates outside.

An attempt has been made to determine who actually might have been members of that Council which, according to "Mark," was summoned on the night of the first day of Passover, A.D. 33, to try Jesus. The attempt is bound to be futile since the Pharisaic transmission remembered only the three or four men whom the Pharisees claimed as members of their sect, or whose doctrines they could place in the chain of tradition that ran from Moses to the last pronouncement of the later academies. Of the seventy-one men who might conceivably have been present, even by probable conjecture we could not get at the names of more than an insignificant minority.

Of the president, the high priest himself—since it is almost impossible to doubt the statement of Josephus that he presided at all meetings of the Council—the little that we can say must be based on conjecture. He is known to us principally through the gospels, and it is as impossible to get a just estimate of his personality from that source as to get a just estimate of the personality of King Antiochus from the books of Maccabees. Outside of the gospels, there are a few brief and casual references in Josephus which do not describe the man at all. Then in the Talmud there is what might be a mention of his son or grandson who was one of the minor doctors of the law.

We must therefore draw whatever inferences we can from the facts. Caiaphas had been appointed by the predecessor of Pilate, the procurator Valerius Gratus. Before him no less than five men had been appointed and deposed in as many years. Caiaphas retained his position for fifteen years. For that, he must have possessed unusual diplomatic skill or else have impressed the Romans, as Herod had done, with the fact that he was their firm and devoted supporter. It is most likely that the latter was the case, and that the procurator even in the five years of his rule of iron had no more approving assistant than the high priest, the seed of Aaron, the man who alone of human beings might directly approach the Lord on behalf of his people. He had so identified himself with the procurator that when the legate recalled the latter he also removed Caiaphas.

Of the priestly majority of the Council a great many must have been like their chief, not merely Roman sympathizers but almost Roman functionaries. Jesus, therefore, if there was a formal hearing, faced a court of nobles to whom he was detestable as a Galilean, as an innovator, as a dangerous agitator, as an anarchist, far more than as a heretic. To the scribes, again, he was an unlettered boor presuming to have an independent right to read and interpret the Scriptures and gaining adherents among the illiterate vulgar by tricks and false pretensions. It is doubtful whether he knew Hebrew at all. Outside of priests and scribes, there were the Pharisaic doctors, some of whom were in all likelihood members of the Sanhedrin. A great many names are reported of a slightly later period, but very few which belong here. That is not altogether an accident. In the last generation before Christ there had been two outstanding teachers, both of them certainly of the class of "wise men." These were Hillel and Shammai. They were in a sense rivals, but their controversies seem to have dealt with methods and with minor matters, and it is probable that they were both Pharisees or with Pharisaic leanings. At any rate they seem to have undertaken systematic instruction and thus to have literally founded schools of the same type as the philosophic and rhetoric schools so common in the region. It is curious that at exactly the same time the two leading jurists of Rome, Labeo and Capito, were establishing schools for systematic teaching.

It is probable that neither at Jerusalem nor at Rome were these schools as completely organized as the famous schools at Athens, Rhodes, or Alexandria; but there was a certain organization after all, and in Jerusalem the doctrines of the "School of Hillel" were opposed to those of the "School of Shammai" at least for the next few generations. The actual heads or the prominent teachers of these schools were almost swallowed up in the schools themselves and the overwhelming personalities of the founders.

Still, the succession to the headship of the School of Hillel is likely to have been vested in his family. His son was Simeon, of whom nothing is known beyond the name, and his grandson was Gamaliel, doubtless the teacher of Paul. The extraordinary veneration in which these men were held was based not only on their character and learning, but also on their lineage. They were popularly believed to be direct descendants of David, and thus of a nobility which made the noblest of the high-priestly clans, or the Hasmoneans, seem an upstart and mushroom stock.

Not all the heads of the School of Hillel can have been members of the Sanhedrin, but Gamaliel almost certainly was and was so in all likelihood in the year A.D. 33.

What would be his attitude toward Jesus? His general reputation was that of a man of leniency and humanity; his Pharisaic doctrine would make him sympathize with the mysticism and other-worldliness of Jesus as well as with the specific dogmas of Baptism, the Kingdom of Heaven, and the Resurrection. There is in the Acts of the Apostles a statement that he vigorously opposed the persecution of Jesus' followers—a statement, however, which may be based on nothing better than the fact that he was the teacher of the chief personage in Acts, the apostle Paul. At any rate, if he was actually present at the trial, not even an arrogant Roman truckler could have as summarily and as brutally hurried a verdict of death as "Mark" reports the high priest to have done. Gamaliel was too great a man for either Caiaphas or Pilate to disregard even in their years of unrestricted power. At this time we may be sure they would be especially unlikely to affront him.

But, as we have seen, "Mark's" version, even by his own showing, cannot be more than a guess. Instead of a hurried night meeting, a harsh and brief interrogatory, a disregard of established rules of evidence and procedure, the trial may have been formally correct, and the judgment even from the point of view of an upright judge just though severe. The high priest certainly commanded a majority, and it would have been as easy for him to have followed the forms of law as to have disregarded them, without altering the verdict he meant to have.

I think we may say that this probably did

happen. If the tradition had uniformly known only of the messianic pretensions of Jesus or his followers, the normal act of the high priest would be to seize Jesus and summarily deliver him to Pilate on a charge which primarily concerned Roman sovereignty. But the oldest tradition contains clear references to another charge—one which concerned "prophecy" and which was based in part on a declaration of Jesus about the Temple. It is practically certain, therefore, that some formal accusation embodying it had been made.

I have said that a passage in Deuteronomy may have been the law which Jesus was charged with transgressing. The Pentateuch was the statute of statutes—undoubtedly valid law. But it is incredible that all the regulations there codified can have been actually enforced in the Jerusalem of A.D. 33. To take a striking example—the "cities of refuge" specifically prescribed in the Pentateuch, had long ceased to exist. We should like accordingly to have something more than the mere fact that a biblical passage could be cited to prove that a particular offense was actually considered capital at the time of Jesus.

Was "false prophecy" such an offense? By

"prophecy," we must remember, we mean not necessarily the foretelling of future events, though that was included, but any announcement declared to be of divine inspiration. We have some evidence that such a charge as "false prophecy" was an important and general indictment, and played a large part in the legal theory of the time.

We have had frequent occasion to consider the Talmud and especially the Mishna, its basic text. This was put into the form which we now have about the year A.D. 200 by a man reputed to be a descendant of Hillel. It is conjectured, and it seems likely, that he expanded and completed an actual book which was a little earlier. But in any case even this earlier book was after A.D. 133—a date which marked so decided an epoch in Jewish history. The Mishna attempted to codify the oral law by subject matter in sixty treatises or "tractates." We may again notice the chronological parallel with Rome. It was about A.D. 130 that the great Roman jurist Julian was organizing and systematizing certain branches of the Roman law in the *Perpetual Edict* and in his *Digest;* and it was about A.D. 210 that the activities of the eminent lawyers Papinian and Ulpian con-

tinued the process which was to establish the
Roman law in the form that ultimately spread
over most of the world.

One of the tractates of the Mishna bears the
title "Sanhedrin," and its general subject is
therefore the procedure of that court. To what
extent may we rely on it? When the tractate
was written, the Sanhedrin had long ceased to
be a real court and was something between an
academy and a religious convocation. The
jurisdiction which it still possessed it obtained
through the voluntary submission of controversies to it. It could not enforce its decrees
except by a sort of ecclesiastical censure, and
it certainly could not have considered capital
cases, much less carry out a death penalty. Yet
capital cases and the procedure in them occupy
far the most important part of the treatise.

Even if there had been records, they could
not have survived the sack of the city in A.D.
70, but there is no reason to believe that there
ever were records. What took place was remembered by those who were present, and it
is such a recollection, weakened by successive
transmissions, rationalized to fit a definite
scheme, and even deliberately modified to suit
an idealized community, that we have before

us. Any statement which might have been due to the process of rationalization or idealization must be received with great caution. So, for example, when the high priest is denied the presidency of the body and that office granted to the *nasi*, the "prince," that is, to the outstanding one of the "wise men," we say confidently that such a statement, in direct contradiction with Josephus, is to be disregarded. Similarly, the statement that a unanimous conviction required an acquittal, a statement ascribed to a teacher of about A.D. 300, can hardly be true. It is carrying to an extreme the idea of leniency toward the accused which the Pharisees made the chief characteristic of their theory about capital cases. It does not sound like a workable principle.

Still, with all these allowances, a certain weight must be given to the persistent iteration of rules which required a strict regulation of procedure in such case. The later Pharisees certainly thought that the purpose of these rules was to avoid a capital sentence as often as possible and prevent the death penalty in as many cases as one could. The original purpose, of course, may have been rather ritualistic than humanitarian, but Judea would be wholly unlike all other communities of the time, if there had been no rules at all.

So we hear that a conviction required a majority of two, that no vote was counted with the statement of the reason for it, that a conviction was invalid unless it was twice voted on successive days, that the convicted man might appeal even on the way to execution if new evidence was forthcoming. These rules, in addition to the biblical rule of two witnesses, are somewhat arbitrarily selected from among the many that are stated, simply because they seem a little more workable than the others, but evidently that is not a very safe basis for selection. Yet we may assume that some of them at least were actually applied in the time of Jesus, and if we accept "Mark's" conjecture, they were all flagrantly violated in his conviction.

The modern notion which rigorously separates the function of judges, advocates, juries, and witnesses did not obtain in ancient times. The judges to some extent partook of all these capacities. Indeed, the witnesses proper had something of the judge's function and much of what is today the judge's responsibility. It seems almost as if the judge by warning could place the whole responsibility on the witnesses, so that the sentence could be made to appear the inevitable result of their testimony.

In the tractate "Sanhedrin" the crime most frequently used to illustrate acquittal cases is, as we should expect, the crime of murder. But at the end there appear several sections that relate to the crime of "false prophecy" or of prophesying in the name of heathen gods. This too was capital, and that this offense was selected for such specific treatment lends color to the belief that in relatively recent times it was still a living law. There is no particular reason, otherwise, why this provision rather than many others of the Pentateuch should be dealt with in such a detailed way.

It is usually supposed that the charge which was brought against Jesus was the charge of blasphemy. That seems to be based merely on the phrase in "Mark" that the high priest cried out "Blasphemy!" and rent his robe when Jesus announced his divine mission. But the word there is a mere exclamation, an ancient practice as common then as it is now, and originally intended to avert the evil of the wicked expression it denounced. It is certainly not equivalent to a formal charge. And such testi-

mony as "Mark" supposes was given did not
deal with any allegedly blasphemous utter-
ances of Jesus but did deal with what might be
called a "prophecy." When we add to this
Christian tradition the importance attached to
"false prophecy" in quite-independent Jewish
tradition, there seems little reason to doubt
that it was this charge and not blasphemy
which constituted what we should call the
"indictment."

The preference which commentators have
shown for the supposition that the charge was
blasphemy may be in part due to the fact that
blasphemy is still an indictable offense in some
jurisdictions and was until recently such an offense in most of them. It was so in ancient
Palestine as well. But the "blasphemy" which
the Pentateuch mentions is a literal cursing of
God or a direct defiance of him. The only pen-
tateuchal reference makes this clear. It is in
Leviticus, chapter 24, and the incident which
gave rise to the statute indicates the character
of the offense of blasphemy in Jewish law. The
half-Egyptian had cursed God—the Israelitish
God—as under the circumstances of the quarrel there described he would have been likely
enough to do. No such thing could have been

charged against Jesus by his most inveterate
enemies.

Jesus, then, we may guess, was formally arraigned of a crime under an existing statute.
The specific act was that he had announced his
power to destroy the Temple, if he chose, and
rebuild it. Was a statement of this sort "false
prophecy"? We cannot be sure, but it is not
difficult to see that it might be so considered.
Witnesses were heard against him. "Mark"
said they lied and that they contradicted one
another. That may be so, but the question
would still be whether the Sanhedrin might
have reasonably believed them. And if we recall what has been said, a court of that time
might feel itself justified in relying on witnesses, since the moral responsibility for a
judgment was largely placed upon the testimony which led to it.

We cannot assume that Jesus admitted he
had used these words. But he probably did not
deny that he had spoken in the name of God,
since his contention must have been that he
was actually and literally inspired to do so. He
denied that his prophesying was false, not that
he prophesied. Whether it was false would
then be the question for the court, and we can

imagine what answer would be given to it by intensely conservative Sadducees whose chief dogma was that immediate communication with God had ceased and that after the prophetic canon had been completed no utterance even of the wisest men had greater authority than that of an opinion.

That Jesus offered evidence on his own behalf is somewhat unlikely. For one thing, he may have had no opportunity to do so. His disciples fled at his arrest is the statement of "Mark," and it is a statement we should find difficult to explain unless it was based on a remembered fact. It is unlikely that witnesses could have been easily found even if opportunity were given, and if, as seems probable, Caiaphas was determined to get rid of the man, we can understand that no very thorough search would be made. The argument from silence is strong here. If any one of Jesus' followers had appeared to testify on his behalf, it is incredible he would not have proclaimed the fact. We should almost certainly know his name.

But it is very likely that even if Jesus had been given an opportunity to obtain witnesses, he would have refused. He needed little to con-

vince him that from the frowning oligarchs before him he could expect no leniency or mercy
—and certainly no sympathy. What would his
attitude be? He was not politically a rebel.
The Roman overlordship in the country in
which he was born and lived nearly all his life
was remote. The direct authority over him and
his had for generations been that of the Herodian family. Above all, Rome and its power, for
all that it seemed so overwhelming, were irrelevant in a world that would be crashing. together into ruin within a few years. But surely
he was not a Roman partisan, and the brutal
slaughter of his countrymen by Pilate some
years earlier cannot have made him love Roman authority as represented in the Roman
procurator.

The atmosphere in which he lived was fiercely
nationalistic and for the most part anti-Roman.
That might in itself account for an attitude of
proud indifference to what such a council as
the Sanhedrin would determine or would not
determine. But probably even more than the
foreign direction of their sympathies was the
fact that his judges belonged for the most part
to the class of the rich and powerful. However
much the teaching of Jesus has been distorted

in the form in which it has come down to us, there ought to be no doubt that one of its most intensely presented doctrines was the sinfulness of wealth. There was no condition so essential to a place in the world-to-come as the repudiation of all the possessions of this world. It may well be that some of the wealthy nobles who sat before him were more incensed at this doctrine than at his religious heresies or the political danger he embodied. And Jesus on his side must have felt himself the irreconcilable foe of the men who in his view could not be otherwise than evil-livers, the selfish exploiters and oppressors of the poor, men who were doomed to imminent destruction by reason of the very wealth which was their pride.

What his attitude was to the "wise men" who formed the minority of the Council is less easy to imagine. The gospels, even "Mark," represent him as the bitter opponent of the Pharisees whom he constantly and unmeasuredly denounces. It may be doubted whether this is historically true. The record was made when Pharisees and Christians were in open and acrimonious opposition and rivalry, and it was almost inevitable that Jesus should be depicted as the conscious foe of the sect as such.

But there is a suggestion even in the gospels that he had Pharisaic friends, and to the Sadducees, the priests, the scribes, he must have been practically indistinguishable from the Pharisees. But in any case the Pharisee members of the Council could not have saved him even if they had wished to.

In the tractate "Sanhedrin" four forms of the death penalty are recognized: stoning, hanging, burning, and decapitation. Evidently no one of these was employed here, and the reason is the one already fully examined. The high priest had no power to execute a capital sentence although his court had the power to pass one. Jesus was crucified.

It was a cruel punishment and a specifically Roman one. But it was not the most cruel of conceivable deaths, horrible as its details are when they are enumerated, and it was not selected or devised as a means of gratifying that hideous pleasure in the suffering of another which is one of the most repulsive and widespread of human perversities. It was not as cruel as the Greek penalty which it displaced and of which it assumed the name, the penalty properly called *staurosis*. This was literally an impalement. Nor does crucifixion compare with the hundred frightful forms of lingering death by torture which Christian Europe invented and used until recent times and which have wrongfully been thought to be justified by ancient example.

It is generally stated that crucifixion was a humiliating death and peculiar to slaves. That is in the main true, but it had become so by accident. The death penalty—any death penalty—had long been abolished for Roman citizens, so that this characteristic and ancient Roman punishment could be legally inflicted only on those who were not Roman citizens, slaves therefore or foreigners. Apparently in earlier days it was freely inflicted on Roman citizens —the highest as well as the lowest—and it contained elements which can be explained only by certain very ancient religious practices.

A man condemned to death was a thing accursed. Apparently it was necessary to get rid of him in some way which would prevent the blight of his curse from harming the community. For that reason he was to be put to death in a way which involved as little bloodshed as possible, since, except in battle, blood was uncanny and there were thousands of superstitions connected with it.

That is to say, this Roman death penalty was really inflicted by scourging and not, properly speaking, by crucifixion. Hanging would have produced the same result, but there was an apotropaic character to the scourging which did not exist in the other. The unfortunate victim was beaten until he was near death, then bound to a withered tree—itself a cursed thing —to breathe out an unholy agony aloft in the air, out of touch with All-Mother Earth and unable to spread his contamination to her. Later the tree was displaced by a wooden gallows which symbolized it.

It is this fact which explains one thing that has always surprised ancient and modern commentators, who wrote when crucifixion had become obsolete. The mere affixing of a man to a cross, even with nails, would not cause death. This would supervene only after several days of exposure and starvation. Yet not only did Jesus die on the same day, but in the many references to crucifixion in older Greek and Roman literature it is never suggested that death did not follow quickly. The statement of "Mark" that Pilate was surprised at the quickness of his death is based on his own account, according to which it occurred in three hours or less. In all likelihood it ordinarily took somewhat longer. But it is assumed that those who were crucified with Jesus also expired on the same day—or rather that they would normally do so.

It was therefore the scourging, in the case of Jesus as in the case of more ancient victims, which was the real death penalty, the actual crucifixion being due to an ancient superstition —a superstition which may equally lie behind the penalties of stoning or of hanging.

The inscription on the cross, as has often been believed, may have been placed there in derision. But that is not certain. We do not know what Roman practice was in these cases, and we do not hear of other such inscriptions. If it was commonly done we may guess that the purpose was also to ward off evil in some way, although the way is not quite clear to us. Perhaps the agonizing man was treated as though already dead and a sort of epitaph set up for him. This would be meant to placate his ghost. We know that practices such as that to deceive the spirits themselves are not uncommon throughout the world. But this is purely guesswork and cannot even be called a conjecture.

The story of the trial and execution of Jesus
has, since his death, filled the whole world, although in his lifetime knowledge of him scarcely spread beyond the petty country in which he
lived and labored. The village in which he was
born disappeared in the wars of the next generation, and its very name has perhaps been lost,
since "Nazareth" comes from the adjective
"Nazarenus" applied to Jesus and his followers, and this adjective may be, not an indication of origin, but a corruption of some other
descriptive epithet.

Those who have read the preceding pages
must have noted how full of doubt and uncertainty most of the elements are which must be
pieced together in order to obtain a picture of
what might have happened. There are few
facts which we can say are certainly established, even in the background of our story,
and almost none that directly concerns it. We
range from a high degree of probability to an
unsupported guess, and our only assurance can
be a cautious self-criticism and a consciousness
of having no preconceived purpose to serve.

Obviously such an examination will satisfy
neither the old nor the new orthodoxy. We
cannot, as the former demands, approach the

gospels with reverent awe, nor yet may we treat all tradition as worthless and deal with the narrative of the Passion as we might with a Homeric myth. We seem to have come to the conclusion that the tradition has much to commend it as to the persons involved in the trial, the date, and the outline sequence of events. These are irrelevant matters for dogma and for faith. For history, they are essential. Traced against the background of the general history of the time, they enable us to re-create the events, no more vividly perhaps than "John" or "Matthew" created it for his readers, but with greater confidence that we shall not be tripped up in contradictions.

One single scrap of torn papyrus discovered tomorrow or the next day in an Egyptian dustheap may well be more illuminating than all the conjectures and constructions we have been dealing with. It is our single chance of better knowledge than constructions and hypotheses.

INDEX

[PRINTED
IN U.S.A.]

www.ingramcontent.com/pod-product-compliance
Lightning Source LLC
Chambersburg PA
CBHW020403100426

42812CB00001B/183